MYSELF

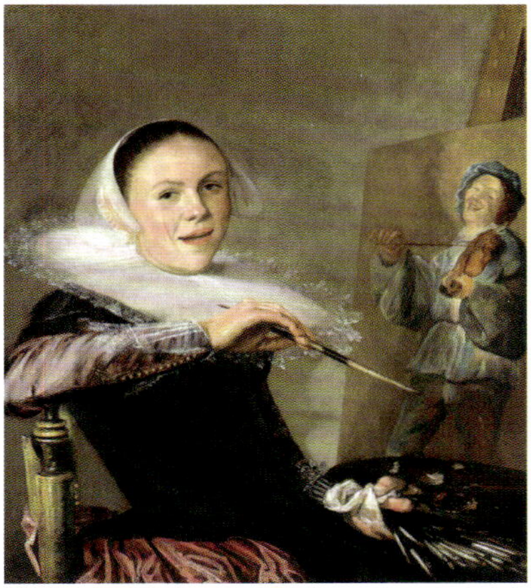

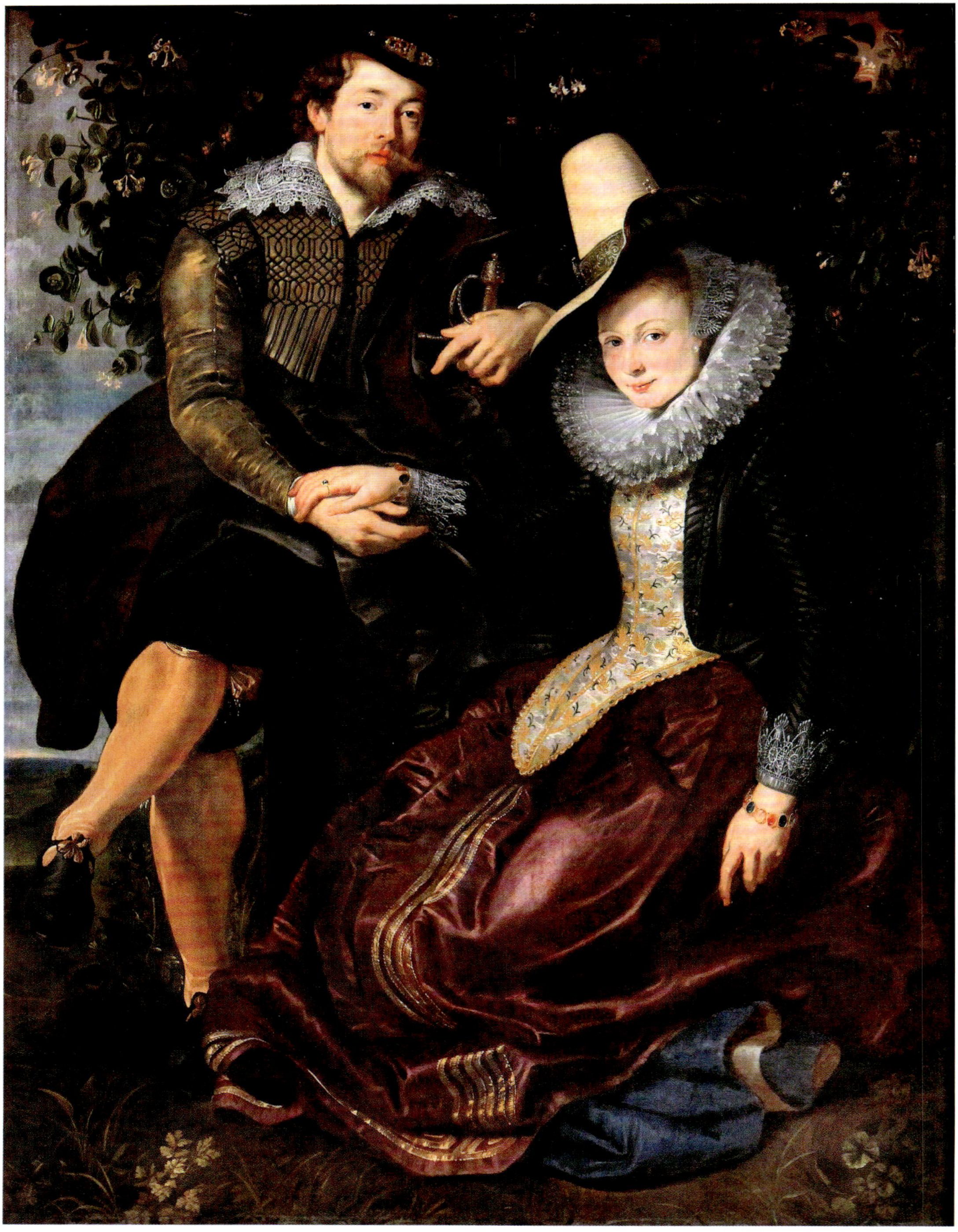

MYSELF

PORTRAITS BY 40 GREAT ARTISTS

JULIET HESLEWOOD

FRANCES LINCOLN LIMITED
PUBLISHERS

Frances Lincoln Limited
www.franceslincoln.com

First Frances Lincoln edition 2014

A catalogue record for this book is available from the British Library.

978-0-7112-3552-6

Printed and bound in China

1 2 3 4 5 6 7 8 9

Front cover: JOSHUA REYNOLDS
Self-portrait c.1779, Royal Academy of Arts, London

Half title page: JUDITH LEYSTER, *Self-portrait c.*1630, National Gallery of Art, Washington

Title page: PETER PAUL RUBENS, *Self-portrait with his Wife Isabella Brandt in a Honeysuckle Bower* 1609, Oil on canvas, 178 x 136.5 cm, Alte Pinakothek, Munich

CONTENTS

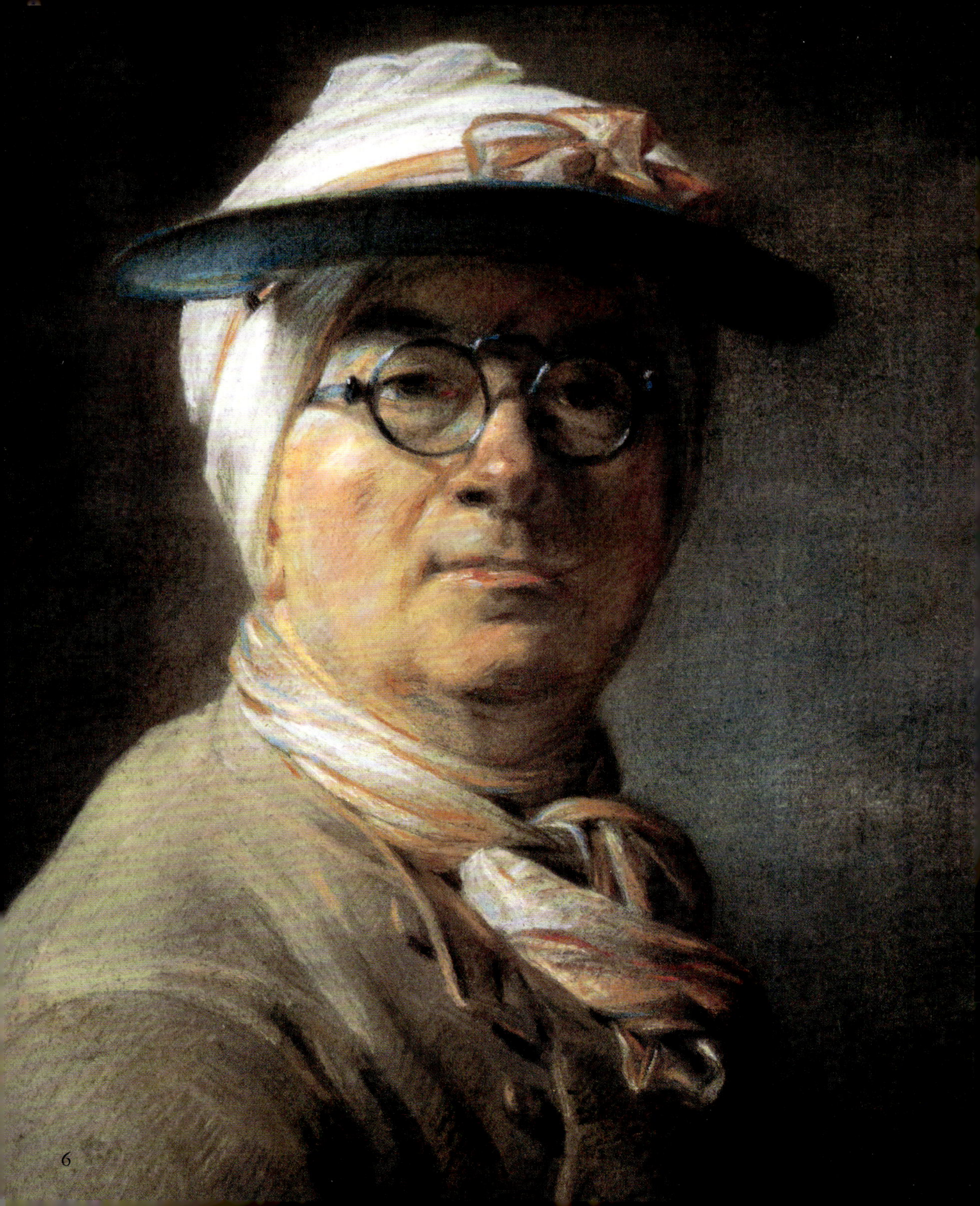

INTRODUCTION

Artists have always required models to sit for them, so they can achieve true likenesses. Once their sitters are comfortable, their features can be examined and reproduced in the medium of their choice. Even in imaginative compositions, where the human figure plays a key role, an artist would still need to have a real knowledge of the way people look to make a work appear convincing.

For years, artists practised portraiture as a means of earning a living. Constable, the great painter of landscape, devoted much of his early career to painting the portraits of people living in his locality. The demand for self-preservation in the form of a likeness, before the era of photography, satisfied the needs of those who could afford to pay for such portraits. Once completed, the finished paintings might hang above fireplaces or in public meeting rooms or wherever the sitters hoped to be remembered.

Self-portraits need not be viewed in the same light. With these, artists become models themselves using their own very familiar and readily available features. To study one's own face or body eliminates the need for a paid model which is far less demanding on the purse strings. This face can be examined simply to keep up good technical practice or even be used as a means of self-expression

The essential tool for self-portraiture is a mirror. Despite the evident truthfulness of the act of looking at a mirror and reproducing what is seen there, a teasing lie takes place. One only has to think of mirror writing to understand this. The right side of the face becomes what appears to be the sitter's left side, were that person to be immediately in front of you. The human face is not perfectly symmetrical. How often do people prefer to have their 'good side' revealed in a photograph? In self-portraiture, because of the mirror image, the face will not appear as it is truly seen by others. This should be born in mind when looking at such portraits.

Rembrandt made a lifelong study of his own face, recording it over time as his appearance gradually changed. He used it as

JEAN BAPTISTE SIMÉON CHARDIN
Portrait of Chardin Wearing an Eyeshade 1775
Pastel on paper, 46 x 38 cm
Louvre, Paris

a vehicle to understand human physiognomy. In his own studio he was at liberty to examine a wide range of facial expressions and to make of these a catalogue of human emotions from jollity to pathos. He was not concerned with flattery. Both Chardin and Goya portrayed themselves wearing spectacles. Was this a reference to their need for better eyesight? Or was it symbolic of the artist's profound powers of perception? Reynolds painted a fine portrait of himself shading his eyes, as if he were seeing far into the distance when in reality his own reflection was very close at hand.

A self-portrait often depicts the image of the artist's face with the eyes staring out at us. Yet aside from the face, all sorts of informative additions can be made.

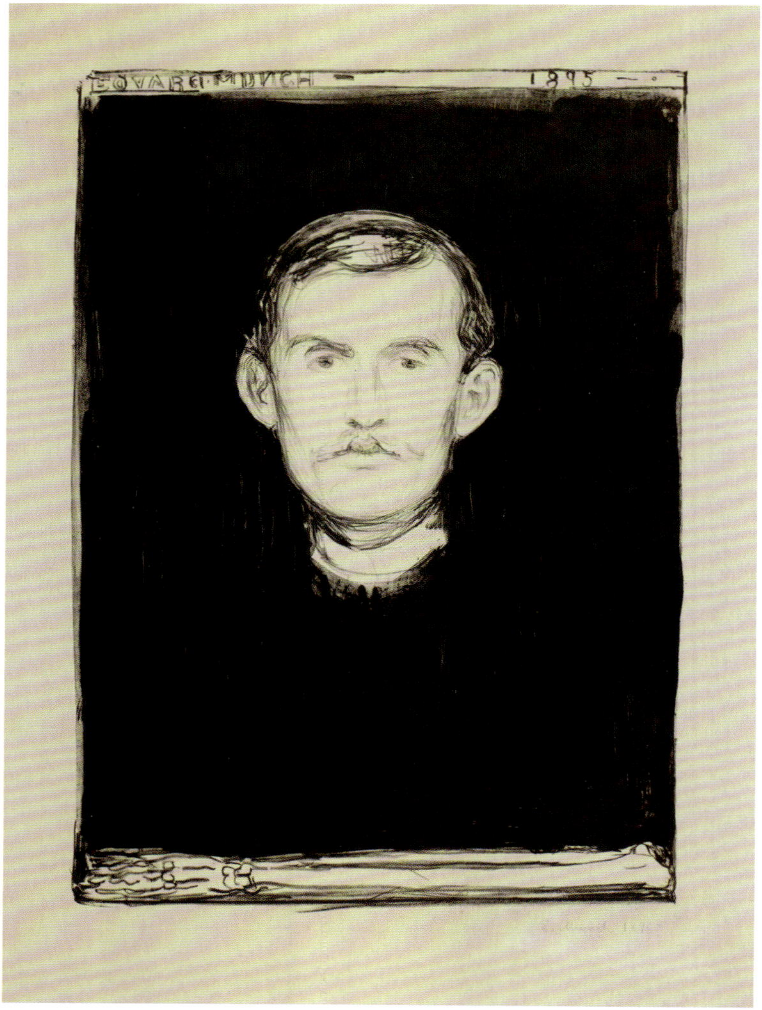

EDVARD MUNCH
Self-portrait 1895
Lithograph on paper, 45.7 x 32.3 cm
Museum of Fine Arts, Houston

Munch referenced the conventional half-torso portrait pose that dates back centuries when he made his striking lithograph. His face appears natural, looking outward, but his arm, resting in the foreground on what appears to be a ledge, takes on the appearance of a disturbing skeleton. It may be read as a memento mori.

The self-portrait can be a form of signature. In early medieval times, monumental sculpture was created by masons who were not considered to be individual artists, but anonymous image-makers. A small ivory dated about 1070 shows not only a signature, but a so-called self-portrait of Engelramnus, the carver himself. Unlikely to be a likeness on such a scale, it does reveal an effort to describe the craftsman at work. By the twelfth century the mason's

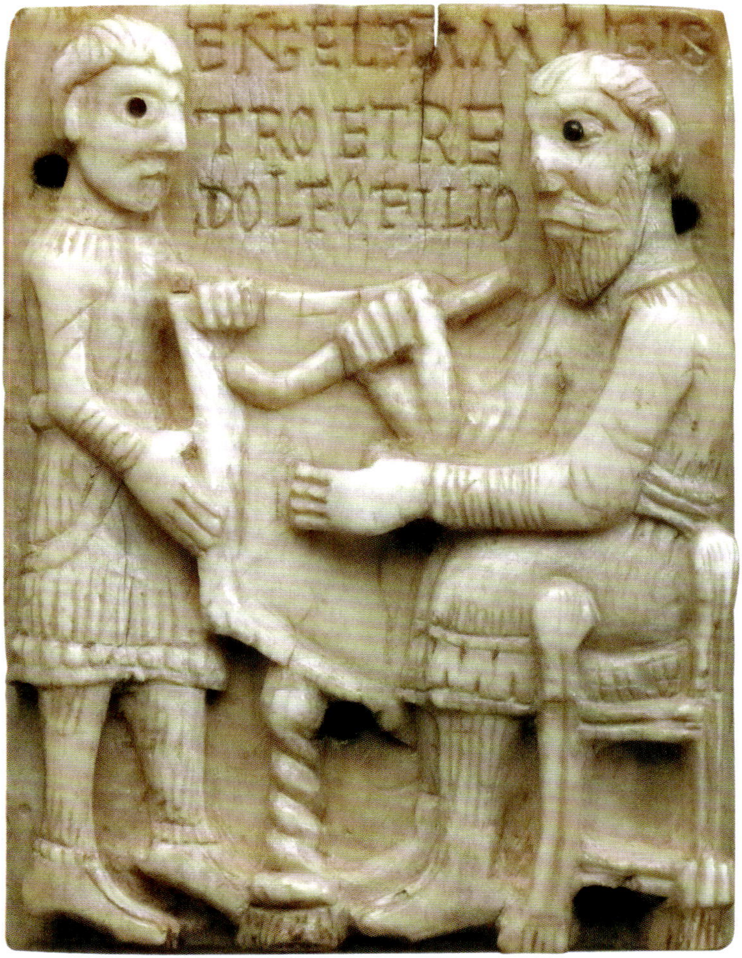

ENGELRAMNUS
Self-portrait c.1070
Plaque from an ivory casket
Hermitage, St Petersburg

status had changed and a written autograph was frequently carved on a capital or lintel as a statement of creative authorship. During the Renaissance, individual artists had earned considerable recognition for their achievements. Having won the competition for creating the prestigious bronze doors for the baptistry in Florence, Ghiberti decided to include his self-portrait within a later pair, the Gates of Paradise. The small head with its distinctive individual features are evidently taken from life.

Self-portraits could be included in storytelling, where a variety of personalities were required in certain populated scenes. Artists were commissioned to create ambitious fresco cycles on the walls of churches or on altarpieces inside chapels. To be given due honour, the patrons themselves or local dignitaries were included as faces within the crowds, usually attendant in Biblical scenes. Artists also distinguished themselves by including their own portraits, with their hands guardedly pointing up to their faces, as if to say, 'This is me, I painted it all.' Botticelli appeared in his *Adoration of the Magi*. The monk, Filippo Lippi, showed himself dressed in his habit as part of the crowd of onlookers in his *Coronation of the Virgin*. These artists did not need to disguise themselves, but actively sought a subtle means with which to be identified with their handiwork.

As further identification, artists added the attributes of their profession in self-portraiture. Their clothing, paintbrushes and palettes were the traditional objects

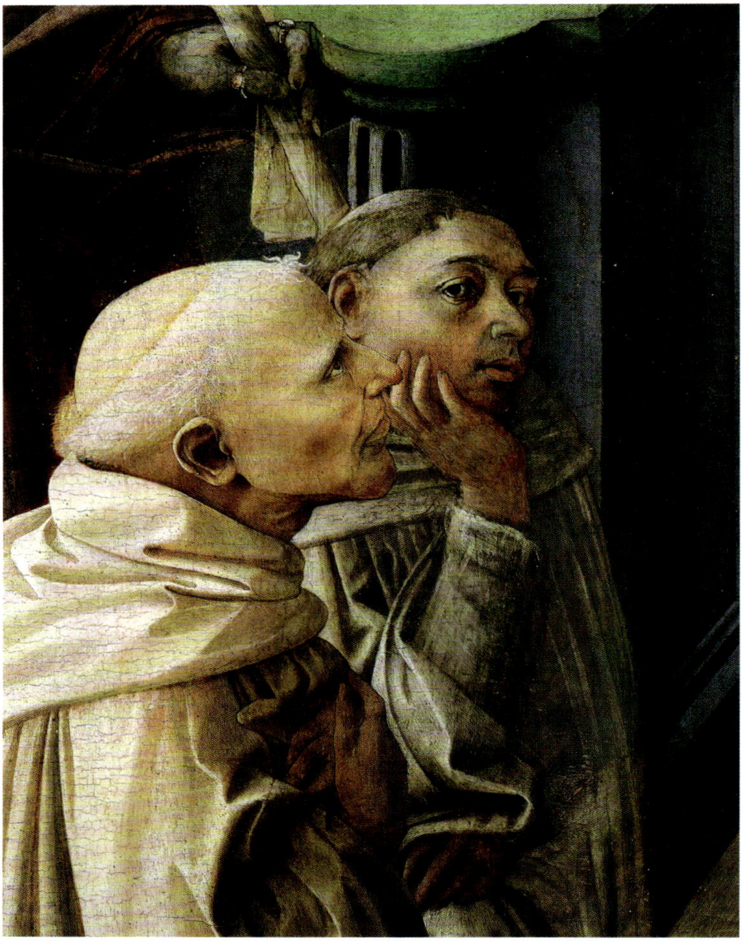

FILIPPO LIPPI
Coronation of the Virgin (detail)
c.1441–7
Tempera on panel, 220 x 287 cm
Uffizi, Florence

associated with their art. Sometimes they showed themselves inside the studio, the world of their creativity, showing the environment in which they worked. The muted tones of Whistler's studio surround the central presence of his model in Japanese style dress. In the background can be seen blue and white porcelain, revealing the admiration he felt for Oriental art. As well as including the attributes of their profession in their self-portraits, artists often made reference to those predecessors they admired. When Reynolds painted himself as the first president of England's Royal Academy, he created not only his own likeness, in fine velvet clothing, but included a carved head of Michelangelo. This was his hero, about whom he rapturously talked and wrote in his famous discourses to students.

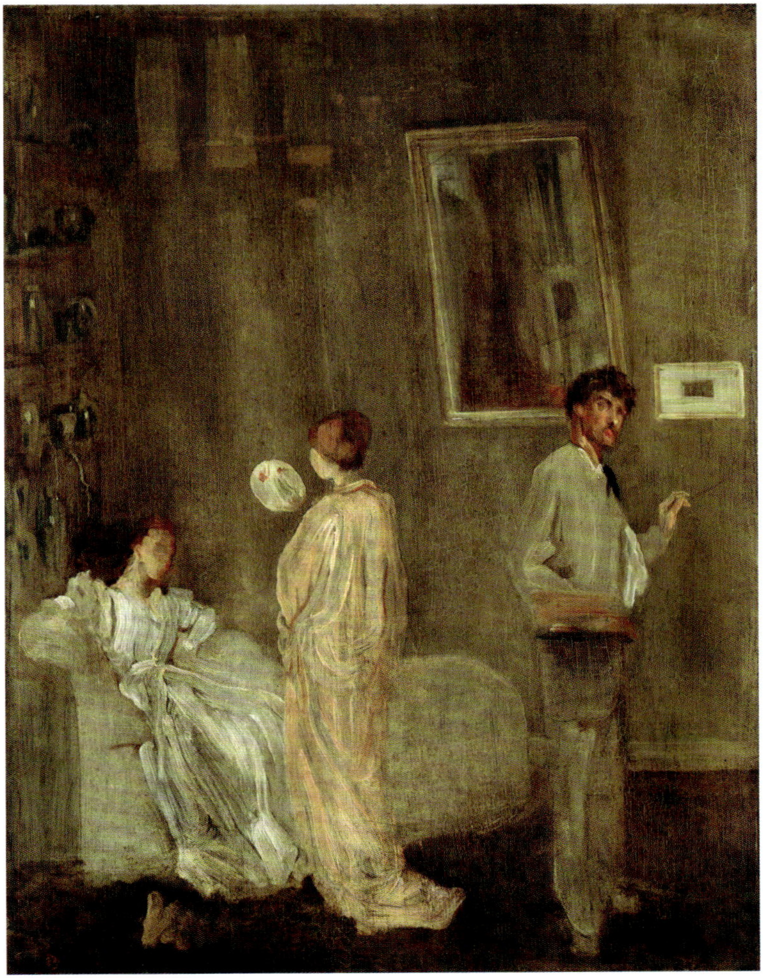

JAMES ABBOTT MCNEILL WHISTLER
The Artist's Studio 1865
Oil on millboard, 62.2 x 46.3 cm
Dublin City Gallery, The Hugh Lane, Dublin

JOSHUA REYNOLDS
Self-Portrait c.1779
Oil on panel, 127 x 101.6 cm
Royal Academy of Arts, London

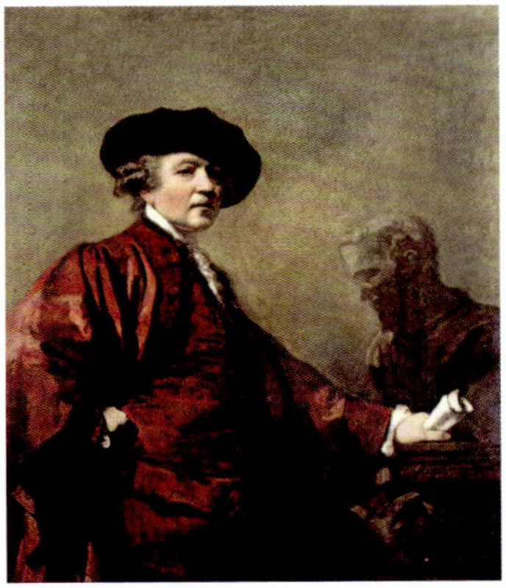

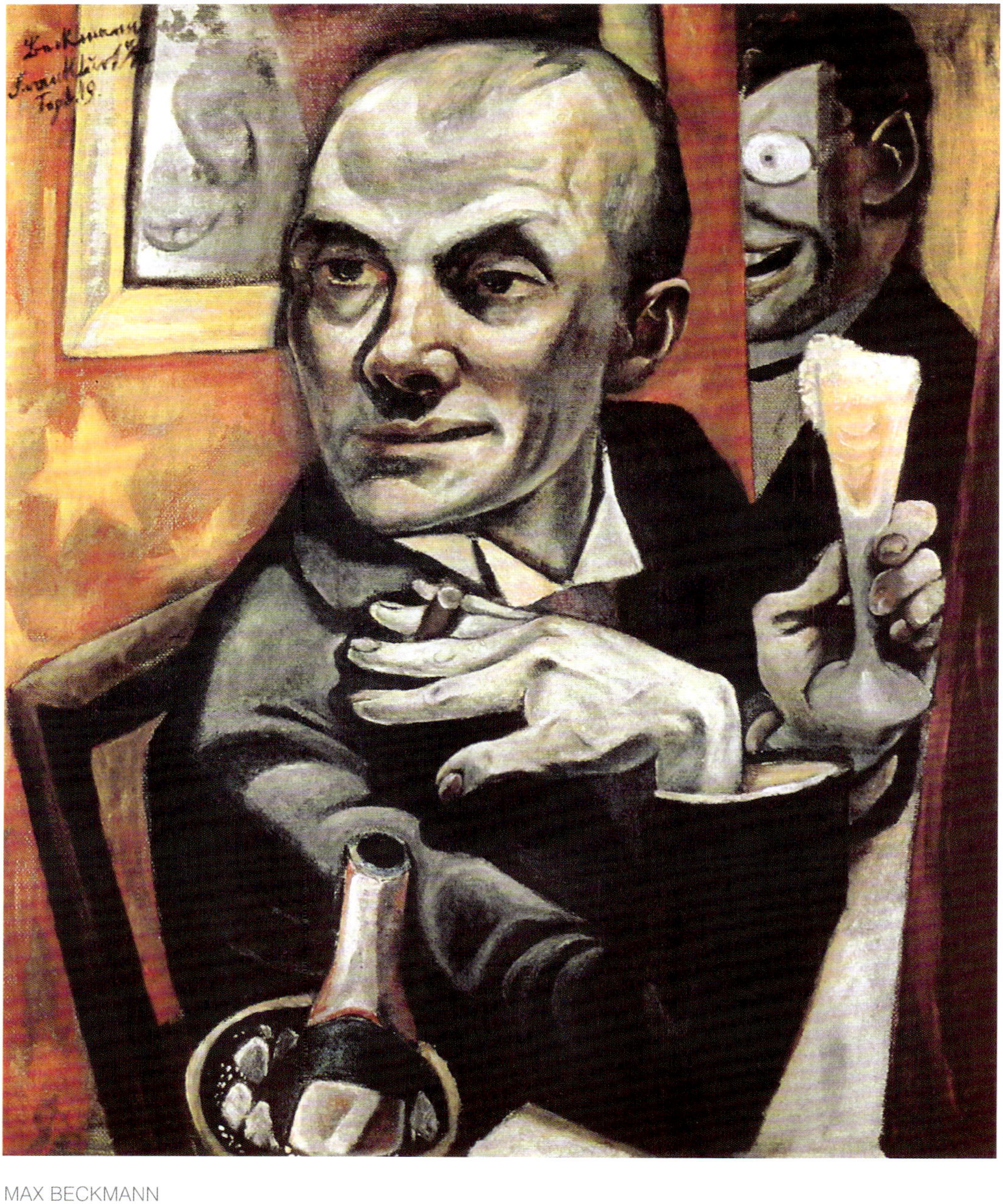

MAX BECKMANN
Self-portrait with Champagne Glass 1919
Oil on canvas, 95 x 55.5 cm
Private collection

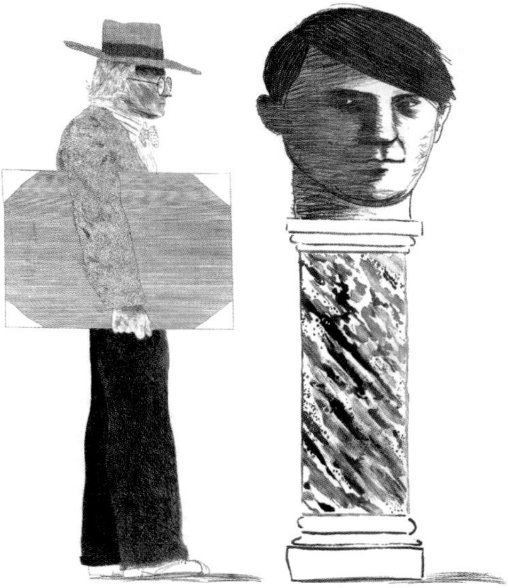

DAVID HOCKNEY
The Student: Homage to Picasso 1973
Etching, edition of 90, 75.5 x 56.5 cm
Collection of the artist

Joseph Wright of Derby portrayed himself in a Rembrandtesque style. Cézanne revealed his admiration for Delacroix when he showed him in *The Apotheosis of Delacroix* ascending into heaven. More earthbound, David Hockney approaches a statue of Picasso, a portfolio of his own work beneath his arm, as if he is about to offer this up to the great Spanish painter.

The self-portraits may not only include professional colleagues, friends or references to other artists, but those much nearer home, the relatives who live at close quarters. Rubens acknowledged the warmth of his own family environment when he portrayed himself with his wife and children (see page 2). Anthony Green painted the most intimate moments of his private life from courtship of his fiancée to their wedding night and into older age.

But artists might choose to show themselves in a more idiosyncratic, self-revelatory way. Egon Schiele made a double portrait where his own two heads seem more like a pair of lovers. Beckmann revealed his penchant for champagne. Bellany painted himself on every birthday as well as in a work following the time he was immobile in a hospital bed. With a seagull on his head or even the head replaced by puffins, many of his self-portraits require no comparison to reality.

There are myriad reasons why or how artists make portraits of themselves. In doing so, they enable us to travel through the looking glass to a world of infinite discovery.

Juliet Heslewood

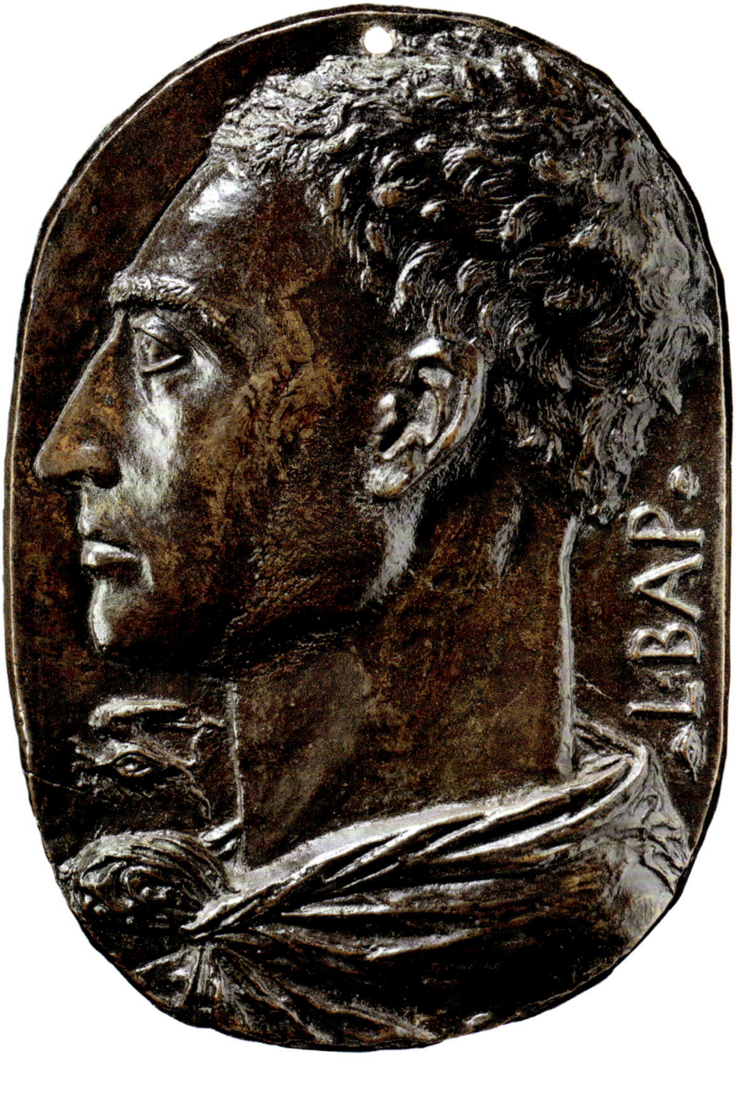

*Self-portrait c.*1435
Bronze, 20.1 x 13.6 cm
National Gallery of Art, Washington

LEON BATTISTA ALBERTI

(1404–72)

Self-portrait

Alberti was born at the beginning of the century that was to witness a definitive change in the progress of artistic achievement in Europe. Known in retrospect as the Renaissance, artists looked to the past to discover new ways of representing the visible world. This rebirth saw the return to ideals of the classical period and the enduring example of Rome.

Alberti became an oustanding scholar and writer, a 'universal man'. His distinguised education led him to pursue all aspects of learning and he referred to great achievements in the past in order to redefine his own era. Though he practised the fine arts himself, it was as a theorist that he became widely influential. In his treatise *On Painting*, written in Latin and published in 1435, he acknowledged mathematics as the basis of art as well as science. In *On Architecture* Alberti referred to Vitruvius, the classical architect and engineer. He dedicated this treatise to Pope Nicholas V who himself dreamed of rebuilding the city of Rome as it once had been.

In his bronze self-portrait, Alberti deliberately chose to represent himself as a Roman, using the medium that was familiar to his predecessors. At the time he was only thirty, yet he is shown with the full confidence that his intellectual pursuits would bring him in later years. His sharp profile reveals a firm, straight nose, a gently furrowed brow and a strong jawline. He is alert, not passive. His angular head is topped by a stylised crop of hair where the curls seem almost mobile. His sturdy, muscular neck separates the lines of his well-defined chin and the folds of his knotted cloak. To the right are the letters of his signature while on the left is a more mysterious sign, Alberti's individual device. It shows a winged eye in flight. The same emblem appears on the back of a later bronze portrait he had made. It is said to represent divinity – the eye that sees all things, distinguishing each one, and therefore having all knowledge.

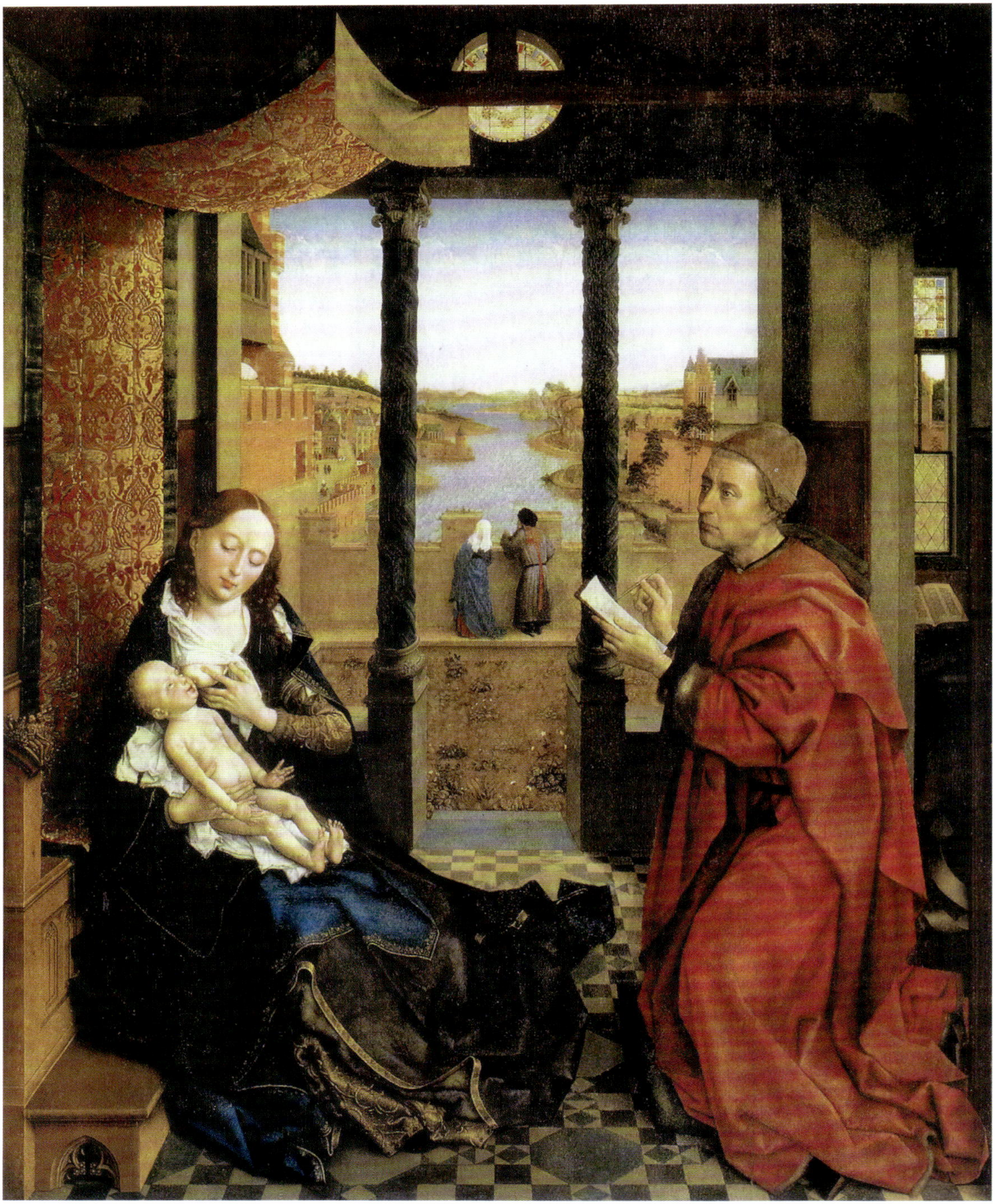

ROGIER VAN DER WEYDEN

(1399–1464)

Saint Luke Drawing the Virgin

As one of the leading artists of the early Renaissance in the north of Europe, Van der Weyden's work consisted mostly of altarpieces and portraits. Images created for worship in churches often showed scenes from the life of the Virgin and it became traditional in Flemish painting to show the Madonna and Child in a domestic interior. The finest detail of objects used in contemporary daily life was achieved through a mastery of the oil technique. Materials such as sumptuous fabrics, intricate wood carving, floor tiles or patterned glass were included in these scenes, revealing the artist's dexterity.

Ever since Saint John of Damascus (born in the seventh century) claimed that Luke had once made a portrait of the Virgin, Saint Luke was adopted as the patron saint of artists. Painters' guilds were named after Luke and as Van der Weyden became the City Painter of Brussels, it is likely he did this painting for the Guild of Saint Luke there.

In his carefully composed work, he shows the two main figures in the foreground of an imaginative and rich interior with views to an outside scene. Two people in contemporary costume stand on a bridge, at the picture's central point, leading the eye, by way of the river, into the distance. Inside, the Madonna looks lovingly at her joyful baby as she breastfeeds. Saint Luke kneels before her and captures her likeness with silverpoint upon paper in preparation for a larger, painted work. Though the Madonna has a conventionally pretty face, Saint Luke's features are more individual. The realism of this face has encouraged the belief that it is a portrait of Van der Weyden himself. By identifying with Saint Luke, who takes on this most significant task, he has drawn attention to his own position as an artist and his commitment to his work.

The painting became very influential and if hung in the Guild's chapel, would have been seen by many artists. Several copies of it are now known but this version underwent infra-red examination, revealing a unique preparatory drawing beneath the painted surface.

Saint Luke Drawing the Virgin c.1435–40
Oil on wood, 137.5 x 111 cm
Museum of Fine Arts, Boston

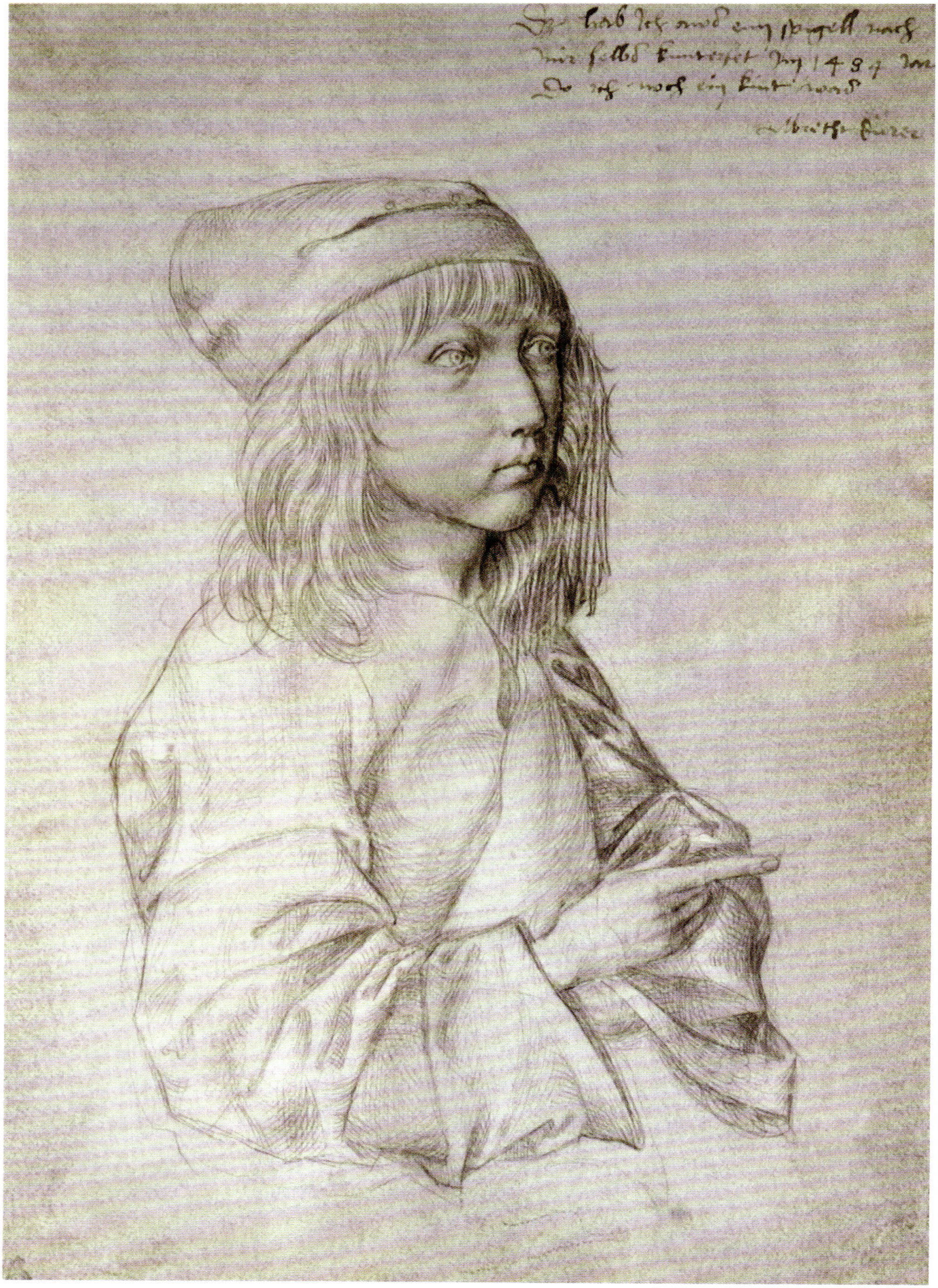

ALBRECHT DÜRER (1471–1528)

Self-portrait aged 13

Occasionally Dürer notated his portrait drawings, pointing out exactly who the sitters were or the conditions under which they were made. His young wife appears as 'My Agnes' and his mother's age is recorded with the date when he drew her, as well as a later addition when she died. In 1484 he made the first of several self-portraits done 'when I was a child' at the age of thirteen, explaining that he had 'put a mirror to myself' in order to do so.

Unusually for a self-portrait realised by looking in a mirror, the young Dürer is not looking directly out of the picture towards us. This seems more like the portrait of some other young boy whose face, in three-quarter view, looks away. He is shown pointing in the direction of his gaze. The gesture of pointing to oneself was a means of identifying the artist, but here Dürer has cleverly separated his real stance as artist from that of the boy he is drawing, who may indeed be pointing to himself in an unseen mirror.

The drawing was done in silverpoint, where a silver instrument, as opposed to any other metal, is used to mark a prepared paper surface. Silver created a fine, grey line with little scope for variance in shading. Using it, the artist's hand needed to be accurate and steady. It was a particularly good medium for small-scale work and became popular with Flemish artists during the fifteenth century. By the seventeenth century its use began to give way to the more versatile graphite pencil.

Dürer began his career learning from his father who was a goldsmith and who wanted him to continue in his own craft. His godfather was an established printer and publisher. The young Dürer's precocious talent saw him accepted as an apprentice to Nuremberg's leading painter and illustrator when he was only fifteen years old. Eventually he became a celebrated painter in his own right, but gained most of his reputation from his fine copperplate engravings and woodcuts which required a meticulous drawing style.

Self-portrait aged 13 1484
Silverpoint on paper, 27.5 x 19.6 cm
Graphische Sammlung
Albertina, Vienna

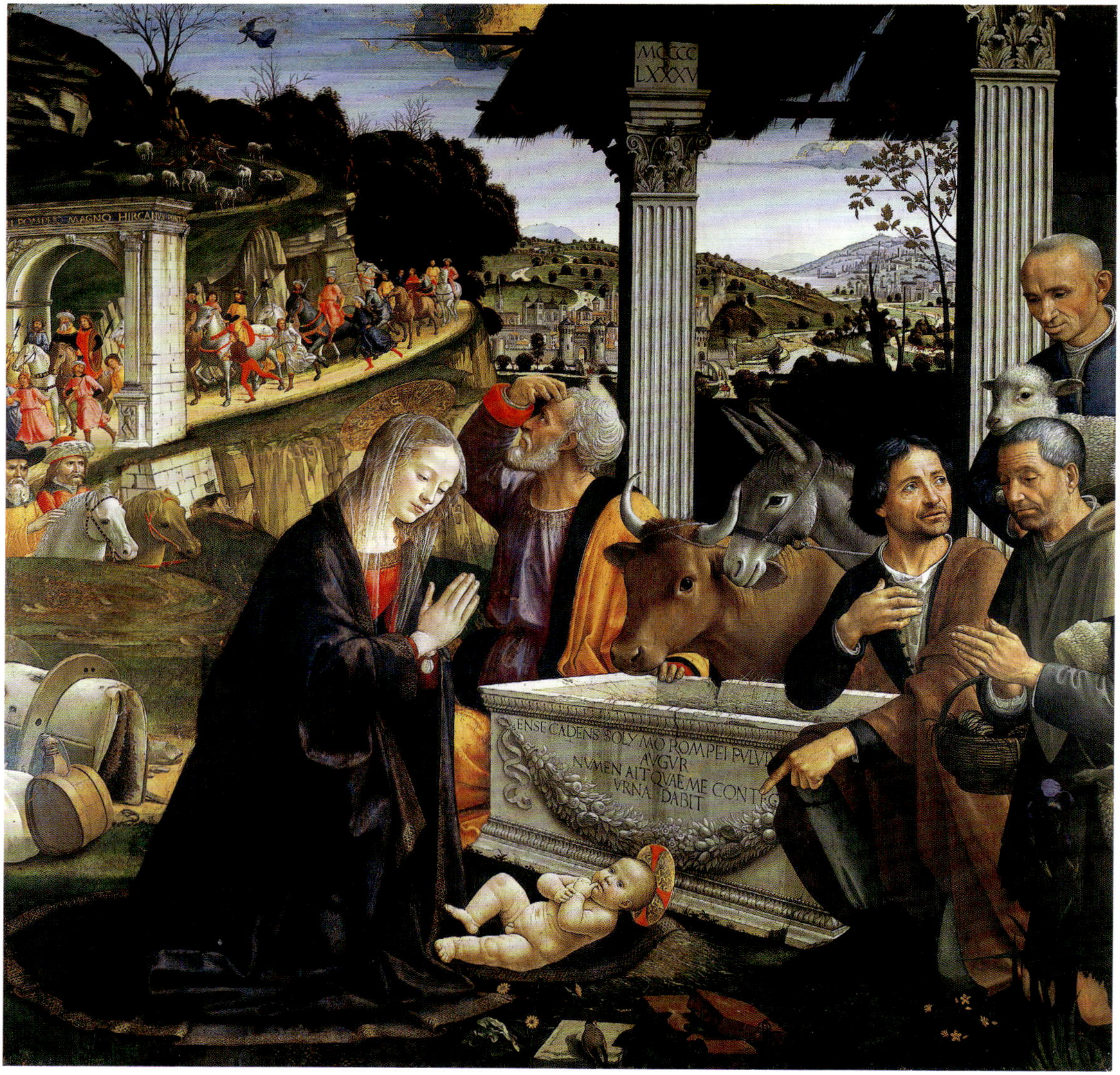

The Adoration of the Shepherds 1485
Tempera and oil on panel, 167 x 167 cm
Sassetti Chapel, Florence

DOMENICO GHIRLANDAIO

(1449–94)

The Adoration of the Shepherds

By the later years of the fifteenth century, artists had mastered many techniques, allowing them to represent the world with a convincing realism. The Italian artist and biographer Vasari looked back with admiration to this period of the Renaissance, a time when Florence had become an artistic centre of Europe. Fine palaces had been built and the walls of its many churches decorated with colourful images illustrating Biblical themes.

Domenico Ghirlandaio was one of the greatest of the town's fresco painters. This technique of painting on to damp plaster was suitable for large wall surfaces. In the limited time before the plaster dried Ghirlandaio managed to create city scenes and domestic interiors with astonishing detail and accuracy. In his large fresco cycles, the narrative scenes of the Bible came to life with true personalities from Florentine society acting in attendance.

The Sassetti family, thankful for the arrival of a son, devoted the theme of their chapel in Santa Trinita to the birth of Christ. Ghirlandaio was asked to paint an altarpiece in the chapel, as well as frescoes on its walls. In his scene of *The Adoration of the Shepherds*, he was able to produce even finer detail by using the medium of tempera, suggesting he was aware of its use in Flemish art. He successfully painted distant perspective, the countryside, architectural detail as well as human likeness. The group of shepherds on the right, in their simple clothing, contains faces that appear particularly true to life. One of these is Ghirlandaio's self-portrait. With his left hand he indicates the Christ Child while his right hand points to himself, as if to say, 'This is me, the author of this painting'. The motif appears again in one of his later Florentine frescoes.

The name Ghirlandaio reflects the profession of his father, a garland maker, and the inclusion of a garland on the tomb, near his hand, acts as a reference to his family. Together with his brother, he ran a large workshop where artists could study. One of his students was the young Michelangelo.

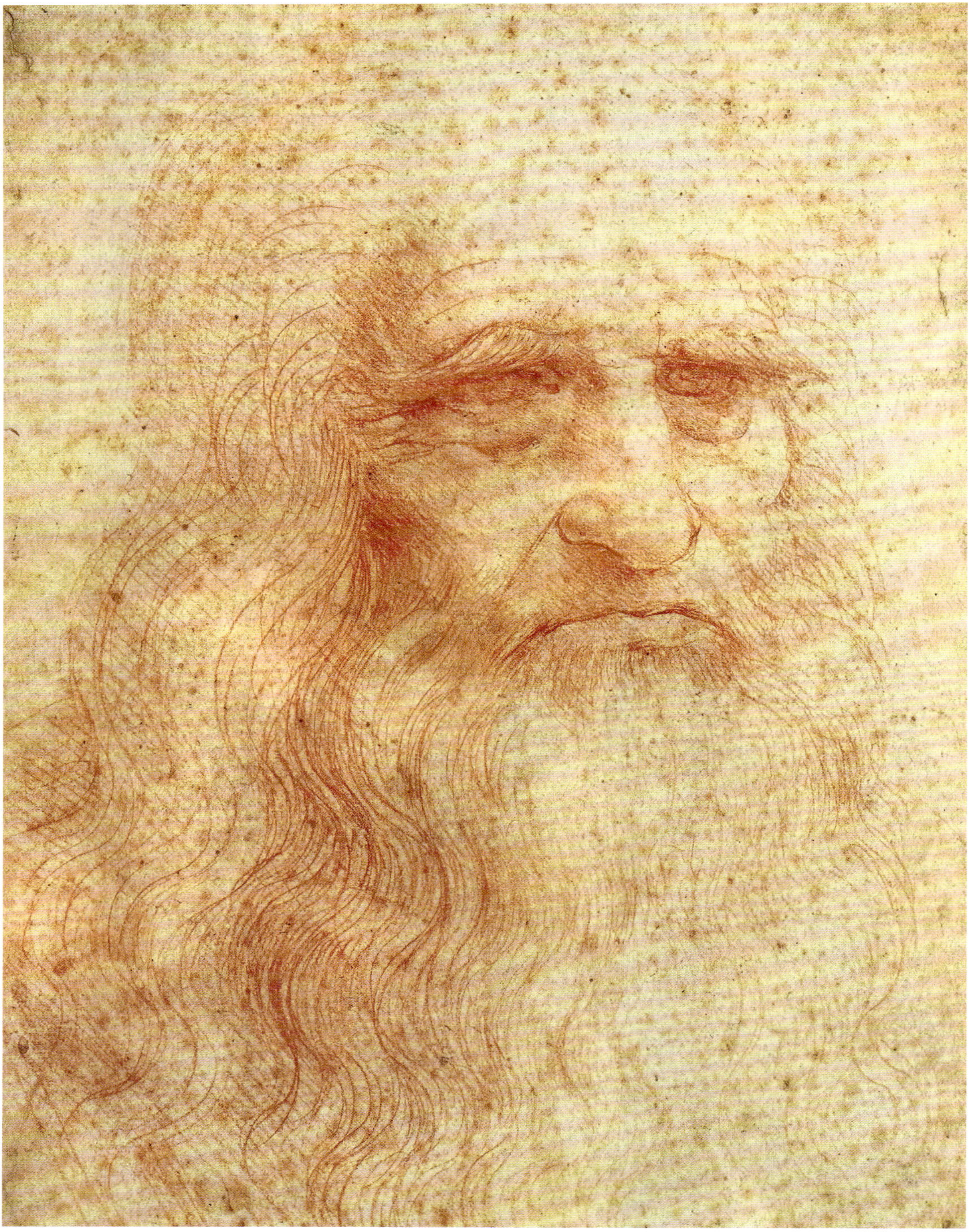

LEONARDO DA VINCI (1452–1519)

Drawing of a Bearded Man

Leonardo was born a few kilometres from Vinci, in Tuscany, where he lived in the house of his father, a successful Florentine notary. By his early twenties, he was an independent artist in Florence having studied in the workshop of Andrea Verrocchio. The biographer Vasari claimed that Verrocchio 'would never touch colours again, he was so ashamed that a boy understood their use better than he did'. At this time Florence had gained its reputation as a cradle of artistic achievement, much being due to the patronage of its noble families, but in the early 1480s Leonardo moved to Milan.

Originally sent by Lorenzo the Magnificent, of the Medici family, to present the Milanese Duke with a lyre, Leonardo's many talents were soon discovered and he stayed. As well as painting and sculpture, he designed weaponry and proposed engineering projects. Over the next seventeen years he was a dutiful servant of the Sforza family in Milan. Later, when the French invaded and occupied the town, he continued to work there as well as in France where he eventually died.

Vasari's description of Leonardo, written within fifty years of his death, claims his work to have come 'from God rather than from human art'. He wrote, 'His name became so famous that not only was he esteemed during his lifetime but his reputation endured and became even greater after his death.' This remains true today. The few paintings by Leonardo that survive are some of the most celebrated and revered in the history of art, attracting countless visitors to the galleries where they hang.

His drawings are less well known. Their fragile nature means they cannot easily be exhibited. The drawing of the bearded man, kept in a vault in Turin, now suffers from 'foxing' – blotches and stains that threaten the paper's survival. But it is generally accepted to be a self-portrait, conforming to descriptions of him. The direction of the hatching, the drawn strokes, suggests a left-handed draughtsman, for which Leonardo is also known. 'In appearance he was striking and handsome,' Vasari said, 'and his magnificent presence brought comfort to the most troubled soul.'

Drawing of a Bearded Man c.1512
Red chalk on paper, 33.3 x 21.6 cm
Biblioteca Reale, Turin

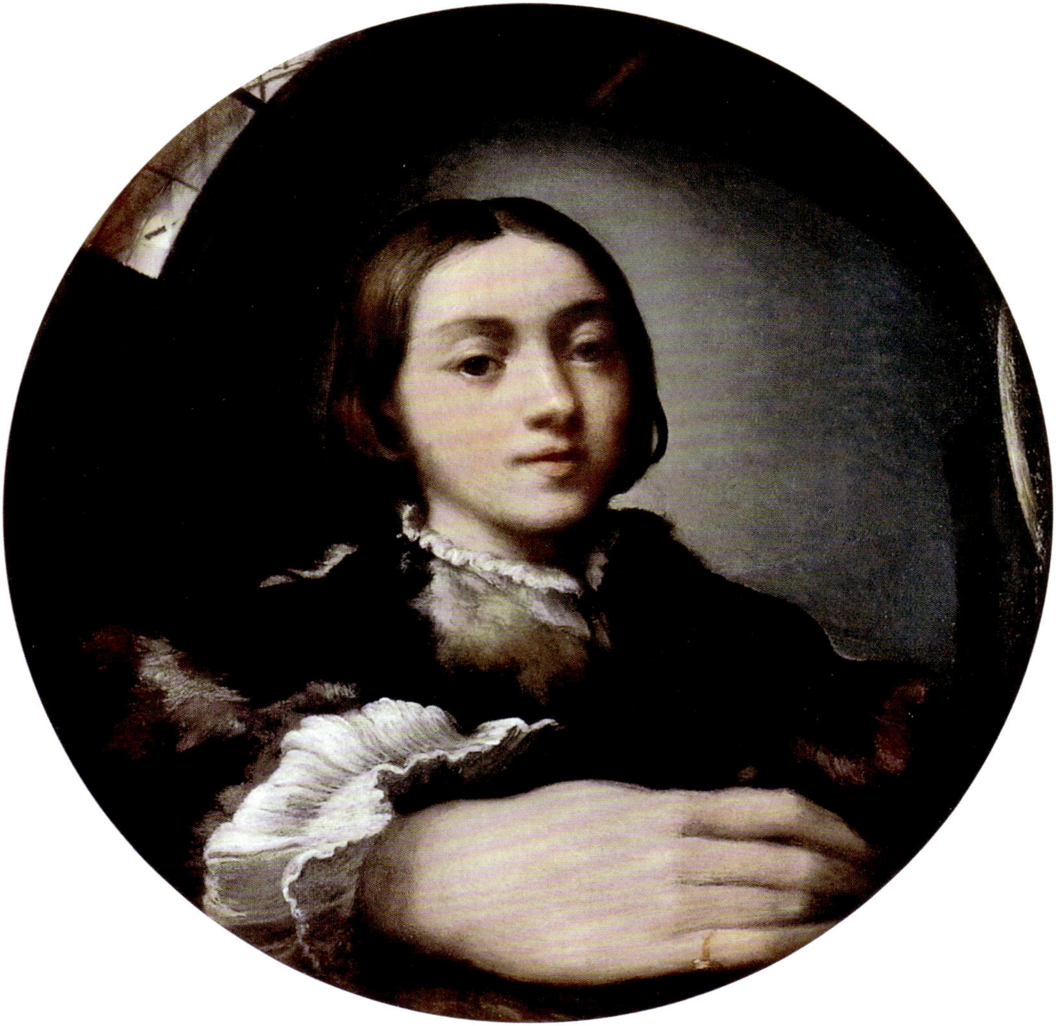

Self-portrait c.1524
Oil on wood, diameter 24.4 cm
Kunsthistorisches Museum, Vienna

PARMIGIANINO (GIROLAMO FRANCESCO MARIA MAZZOLA) (1503–40)

Self-portrait

Vasari claimed that the young artist known as 'the little one from Parma', travelled to Rome to acquire the patronage of Pope Clement VII. With him he took three paintings, including the self-portrait said to be his reflection in a barber's mirror. 'So happily, indeed, did he succeed in the whole of this work,' Vasari wrote, 'that the painting was no less real than the reality, and in it were seen the lustre of the glass, the reflection of every detail, and the lights and shadows, all so true and natural, that nothing more could have been looked for from the brain of man.' The Pope was suitably 'struck with astonishment' and Parmigianino was given several commissions in the Holy City.

His frescoes and altarpieces are in the Mannerist style, a term that was originally used in the seventeenth century in a perjorative sense. To reproduce the world as we see it, in three dimensions, on a two-dimensional surface such as a canvas, was one of the great achievements of the earlier Renaissance period. An understanding of perspective lay at the root of this realistic representation. But in creating this small panel (which itself is carved in imitation of the mirror's convex shape) Parmigianino was deliberately evoking the very meaning of 'art', which is not reality, but artifice.

Though he became deeply interested in alchemy, on a more professional level he was fascinated by science and illusions made by the human eye. Together with other Mannerist painters, he exaggerated certain appearances. One of his later paintings is entitled *Madonna with the Long Neck* and shows his preference for distorting the human figure for dramatic or emotional effect. In his self-portrait his hand is so close to the mirror's edge that it becomes larger than his face. Yet this hand belongs to him and is the source of his creativity. In the room behind, also distorted, the gold frame of his imitation mirror, upon which he is working, is seen on the right.

The painting, which was given to the Pope, was always owned by prestigious admirers and finally reached the collection of the Habsburg royal family in Vienna.

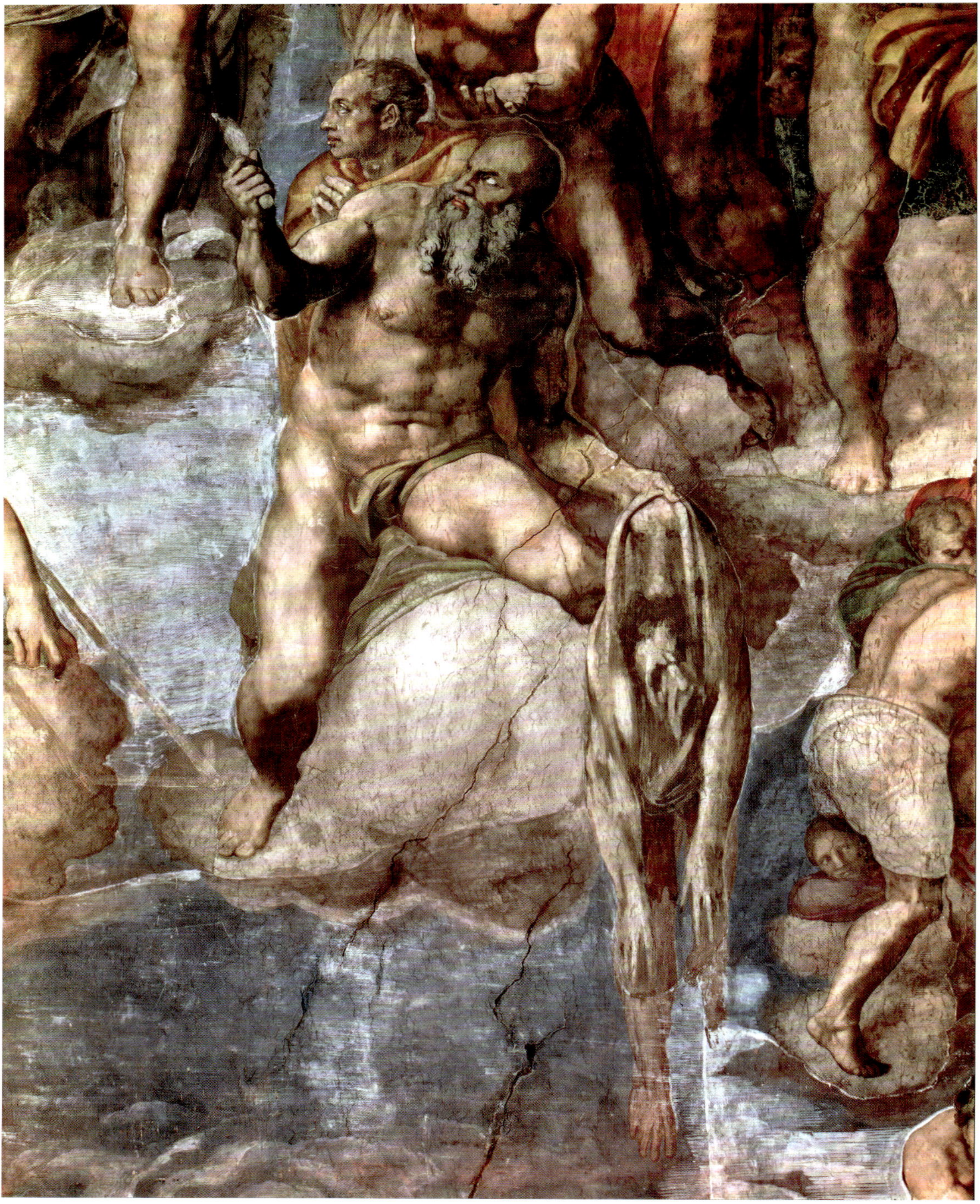

MICHELANGELO BUONARROTI (1475–1564)

The Last Judgement

'The man whose work transcends and eclipses that of every other artist, living or dead, is the inspired Michelangelo Buonarroti, who is supreme not in one art alone, but in all three.' Vasari, who knew Michelangelo, described him in the context of the achievement of the High Renaissance when a rebirth of the arts, rivalling ancient times, was considered to have reached its peak. As painter, sculptor and architect, Michelangelo's extraordinary career elevated him to the stature of a genius with qualities that approached the 'divine'. His early years were spent in Florence but it was for the papacy in Rome, with commissions that demanded an almost super-human effort, that he gained his lasting reputation.

Pope Julius II asked Michelangelo to create a vast stone monument as his tomb. For nearly forty years Michelangelo, who considered himself a sculptor first, struggled with this while working on other commissions, including the Sistine Chapel ceiling, also for Julius. Nearly thirty years later he returned to the chapel to paint the entire surface of the wall behind the altar. Since the early medieval period the Last Judgement had reminded congregations of the journey of their souls after death. It was a subject loaded with dramatic possibilities, but Michelangelo's version reveals his preoccupation with the sculptural form and expressive potential of the human body.

Christ rises above a dense mass of naked limbs, torsos and heads that move about him, suspended in space. Immediately below Christ are two saints who carry the objects of their martyrdom. Their prominent place links them to the feast days associated with the chapel's construction. Saint Lawrence holds an iron grid while Saint Bartholomew, who was flayed, holds his own drooping flesh in which a face appears. This face is said to be Michelangelo's self-portrait

Michelangelo composed a great deal of poetry in which his personal thoughts were given a form of expression comparable to the other arts he practised. Late in his life he wrote: 'Not painting nor sculpture can quieten/ my soul that now turns toward His holy love/ whose arms opened on the cross to take us in.'

The Last Judgement (detail of Bartholomew holding his flayed skin) 1538–41
Fresco, Sistine Chapel Ceiling, Vatican Museums and Galleries, Vatican City, Rome

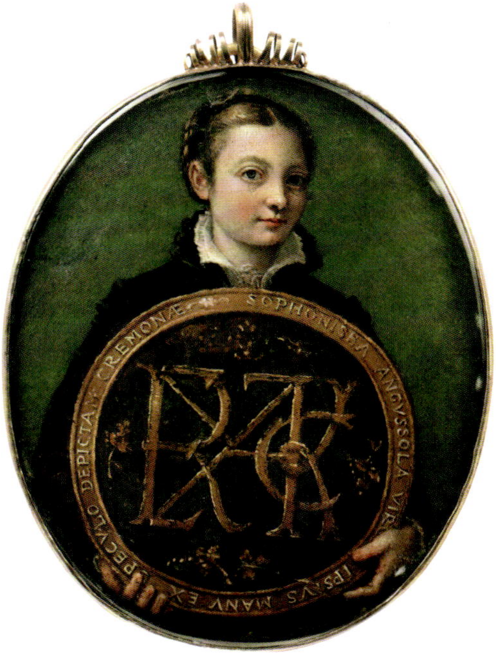

Self-portrait *c.* 1556
Varnished watercolour on parchment, 8.3 x 6.4 cm
Museum of Fine Arts, Boston

SOFONISBA ANGUISSOLA

(1532–1625)

Self-portrait

Sofonisba, like her five sisters and brother, received a good education. They were said to be descended from a Carthaginian family. Her name was that of a famous heroine from Carthage who had bravely poisoned herself, rather than suffer humiliation from the Romans. In a small miniature, Sofonisba proudly holds a medallion like a shield, upon which her father's name is entwined in a monogram. Around the edge a Latin inscription explains that she, a virgin from Cremona, has used a mirror to create the painting. So she confirms the truth of the likeness. Other early self-portraits show her with similarly large round eyes and neat hair plaited round her head.

She had a remarkable career. She studied with established artists and showed that women could set out in a male-dominated profession and achieve an equal footing. In Rome she met Michelangelo who was impressed by her proficiency. Her reputation gained her acceptance in the Spanish court of Philip II to teach his wife, Elizabeth de Valois, and to act as her lady-in-waiting. There she produced fine, formal portraits of his entourage. Philip wanted to ensure a noble marriage for her and in this she was not discouraged from her work. When she was forty-seven her husband died but while sailing home towards Cremona, she met the ship's captain, a Genoese nobleman, whom she married the following year. She continued painting and was once visited by Van Dyck who made a sketch of her. She gained international recognition for her portraiture and Vasari acknowledged that 'by herself she made some very rare and very beautiful paintings'.

The old lady (aged seventy-eight) in the self-portrait of later years shows Sofonisba in the kind of pose reminiscent of many of her sitters. Her husband, on what would have been the hundredth anniversary of her birth, placed an inscription on her tomb that described her as 'among the illustrious women of the world, outstanding in portraying the images of man. Orazio Lomellino, in sorrow for the loss of his great love, in 1632, dedicated this little tribute to such a great woman.'

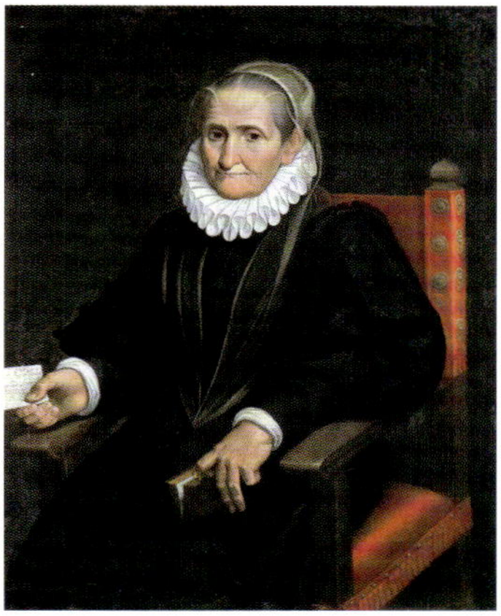

Self-portrait as an Old Woman 1610
Oil on canvas, 96.5 x 76 cm
Kunsthaus, Zurich

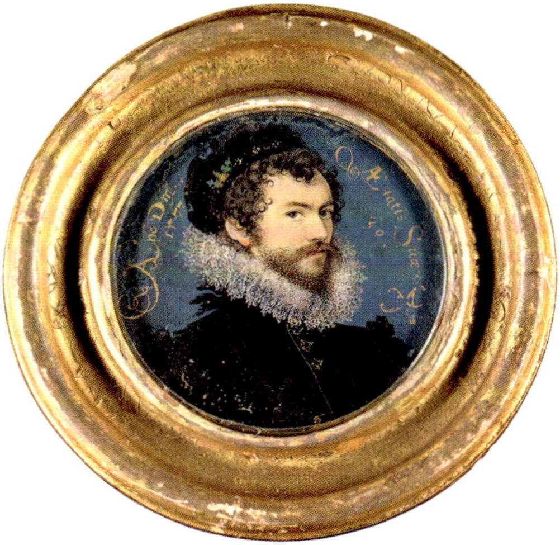

Self-portrait aged 30 1577
Watercolour on vellum 4.1 cm diameter
Victoria and Albert Museum, London

NICHOLAS HILLIARD (1547–1619)

Self-portrait aged 30

By the time he was thirty, Nicholas Hilliard was already an esteemed painter in the court of Queen Elizabeth I. Though he made two half-length panels of the Queen, it is as a limner, or miniature painter, that he gained his lasting reputation. He had trained as a limner and goldsmith with his father and was apprenticed to the Queen's jeweller whose daughter he later married. For a few years he worked in France, where he painted this self-portrait. On returning to England he received an annual allowance from the Queen.

Painting in miniature had been practised since the middle ages with the development of manuscript illumination. Holbein, who was working in England from 1526, made several versions of his large paintings on a much smaller scale. In the hands of Hilliard the miniature portrait came into its own. He used little variance from bright light to shade, lending the sitter's face great clarity. The Queen is said to have preferred to pose outside, where no shadows fell. As in his other portraits, he showed himself against a plain, uncluttered background, his pale face surrounded by the delicate finery of his clothes. The precision with which he used his tiny brush helped to reveal each detail – a jewel, a piece of lace, the hairs that make up a single curl. On either side of his head he wrote in Latin 'Year of Our Lord 1577' and 'At the Age of 30' together with his initials.

He was a contemporary of Shakespeare and his famous painting *A Young Man Among Roses* has been associated with the writer's romantic heroes. It may be a portrait of the Earl of Essex, a favourite of the Queen. Hilliard went on to become painter to James I. He decided to write a *Treatise Concerning the Arte of Limning* in which he described not only his painting methods and the importance of drawing, but also much about his own temperament. This exposure of his work helped raise an awareness of the artist's role as more than that of a craftsman. He believed that 'of all things the perfection is to imitate the face of mankind'.

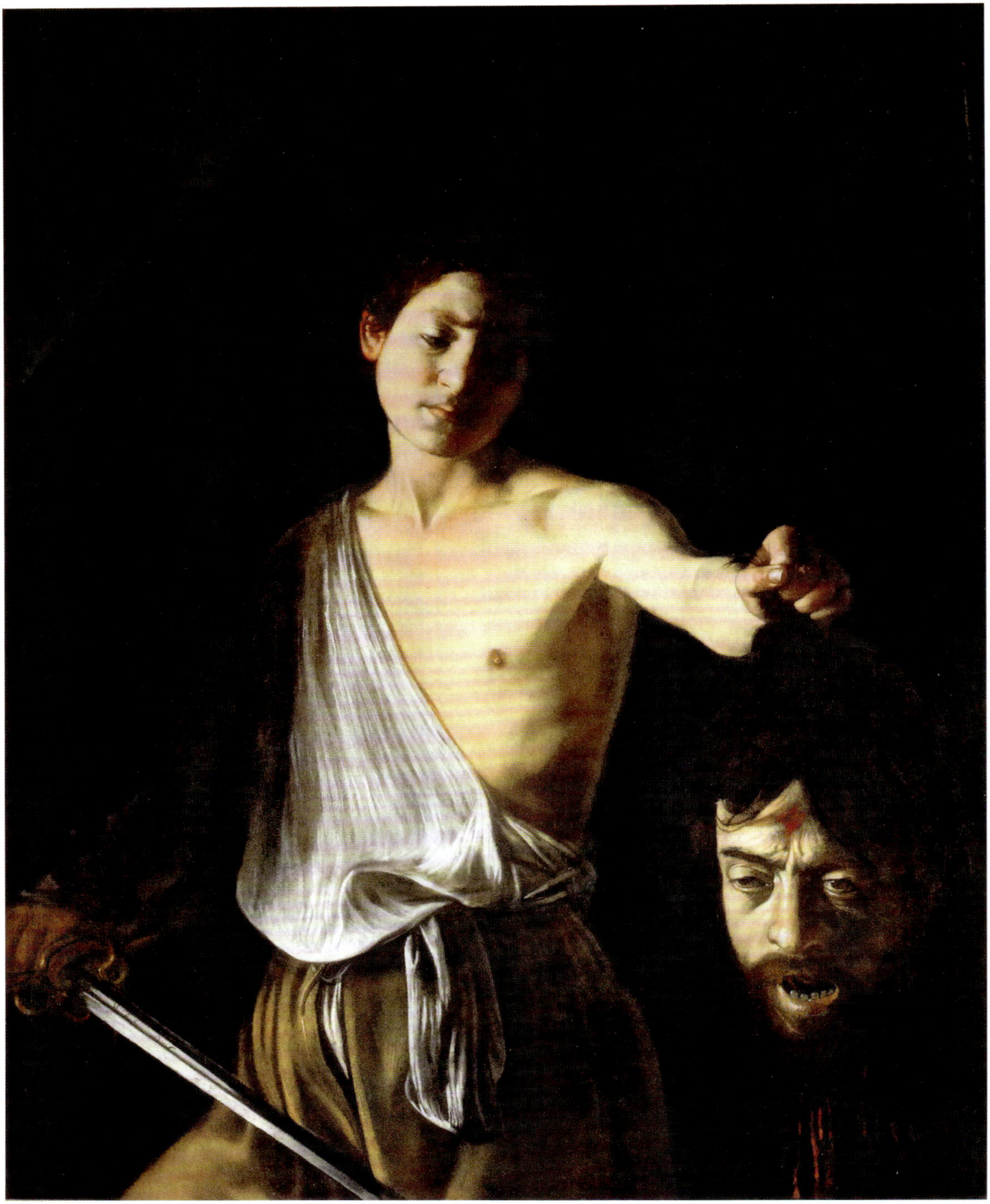

CARAVAGGIO (1571–1610)

David with the Head of Goliath

When he arrived in Rome, the young painter Caravaggio found the city risen up against Protestantism. During the Counter Reformation, the Catholic Church sought every means to return to its former power. By building splendid new places of worship, with lavish decoration that might inspire faith, the Popes and their clergy encouraged artistic endeavour.

Earlier in the century, Michelangelo had also worked in Rome and had achieved the kind of fame that set him above all other artists of his generation. Caravaggio adopted the name of the village near Milan where he and his family had moved. His own work was to gain him a mixed reputation, much due to his provocative and highly original style. Caravaggio became a master of light. The single, unseen light sources that illumine the scenes of his religious works, gave them a dramatic sense of occasion as well as a profound spirituality. Their startling transition from brightness to dark, with little gradation between, meant figures were singled out, as if with a spotlight. His models were often people he found in the rough areas of the city he frequented. The realism with which he painted them was another mark of his originality, though at the time frequently frowned upon.

He placed his own striking face in several canvasses, but the use of his self-portrait as the decapitated head of Goliath was a daring move. The Old Testament story was often thought to represent Christ slaying Satan. Here his head is hideous, so freshly dead the mouth seems still to contain speech while the eyes appear to retain a vision of his fate. Blood from his neck drips into the darkness. David's expression is a remarkable mixture of disgust and compassion.

Caravaggio's life was as dramatic as his work. He was known to have committed murder. This painting was intended for the pope's nephew, Scipione Borghese, who was the chief administrator of papal justice and the person who might have influenced Caravaggio's punishment. The artist's last years were spent in exile, the circumstances of his death while on the run, still uncertain.

David with the Head of Goliath 1606
Oil on canvas,
125 cm x 101 cm
Galleria Borghese, Rome

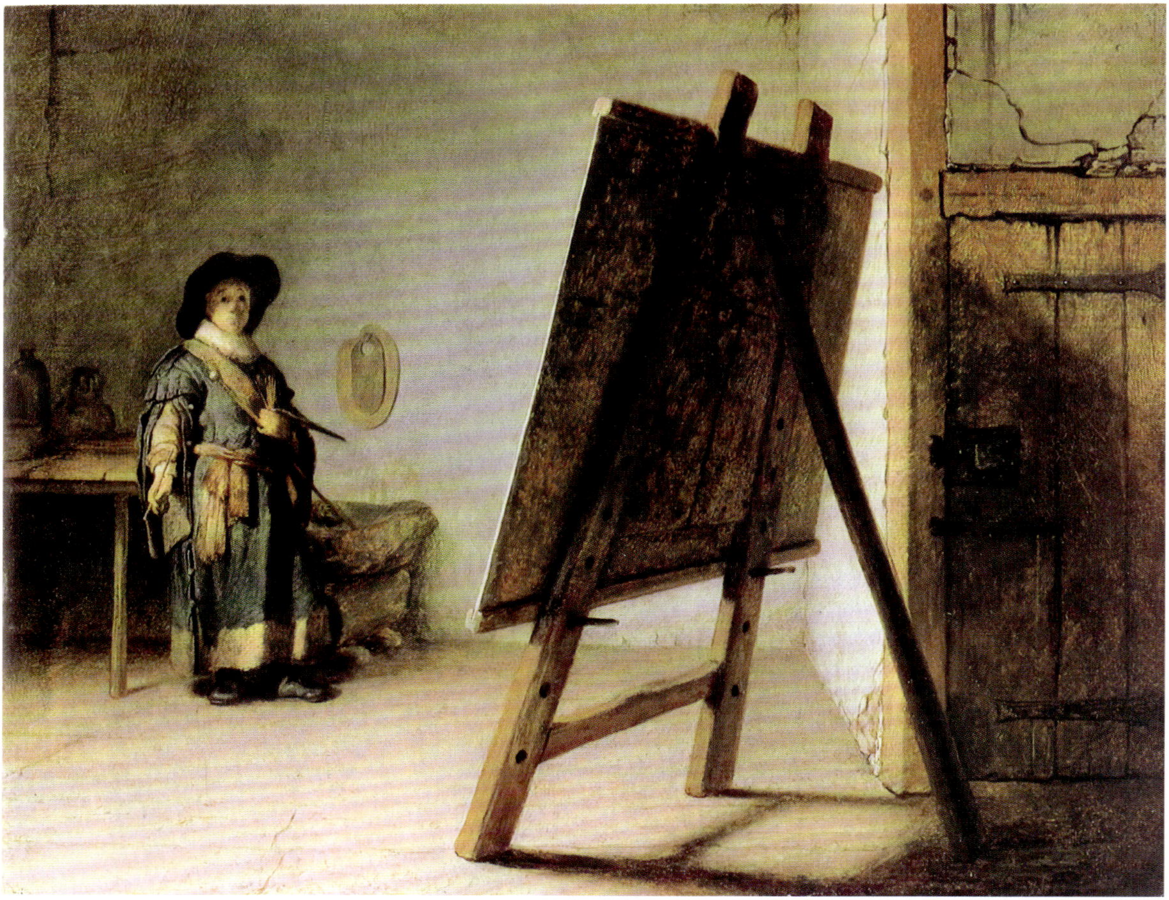

The Artist in His Studio c.1630
Oil on panel, 25 cm x 31.5 cm
Museum of Fine Arts, Boston

REMBRANDT VAN RIJN (1606–69)

The Artist in His Studio

Throughout his life, Rembrandt examined his own face. The result of his studies is an extraordinary visual catalogue of the ageing process of one individual person. His technique of using layer upon layer of oil pigment, often in a thin sweep of dry impasto, lent itself to the description of flesh. Whether he is shown laughing or pensive, his characteristic use of a single source of light enhanced the poetic aspects of his self-portraits.

The painting of the young artist in his studio reveals Rembrandt's ability to manipulate oil paints in order to differentiate various types of material. Though the room is bare, he brings interest to the textures of the crumbling plaster on the walls, the floorboards, the door, as well as his own clothing. The artist stands poised with his brushes in a shaded corner of the room, a diminutive figure distanced from the large, illumined canvas by a wide empty space. A moment in time is caught as he reflects upon his next move, perhaps with trepidation.

One of several self-portraits painted towards the end of his life daringly shows his old face in close-up. Rembrandt frequently used a palette of reduced colours that made up the flesh tones of his face. They are repeated in his beret. Spreads of white impasto highlight part of his brow, his thin, wispy curls and the neckline of his clothes. Similar dry brushstrokes have been moved over the canvas to give shape to his facial features without defining them too sharply. His flesh hangs from his cheek to meet his double chin. Darkness surrounds him.

Nearly one hundred self-portraits are known of Rembrandt but to further his career he was committed to painting portraits of others as well as Biblical and historical subjects. For these he needed to create his own descriptive vocabulary to illustrate specific narrative events. Gestures, facial expressions and unusual lighting effects all contributed to the drama of his brilliantly realised scenes. Though he also made landscape paintings and engravings, he is remembered for the profound humanity that infused so many of his figurative works.

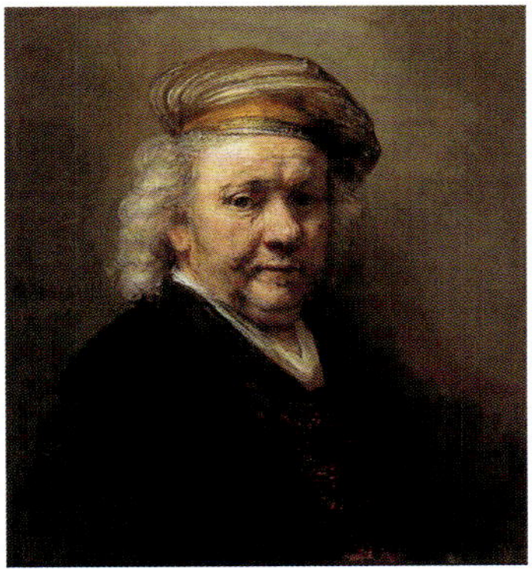

Self-portrait 1669
Oil on canvas, 63.5 x 57.8 cm
Mauritshuis, The Hague

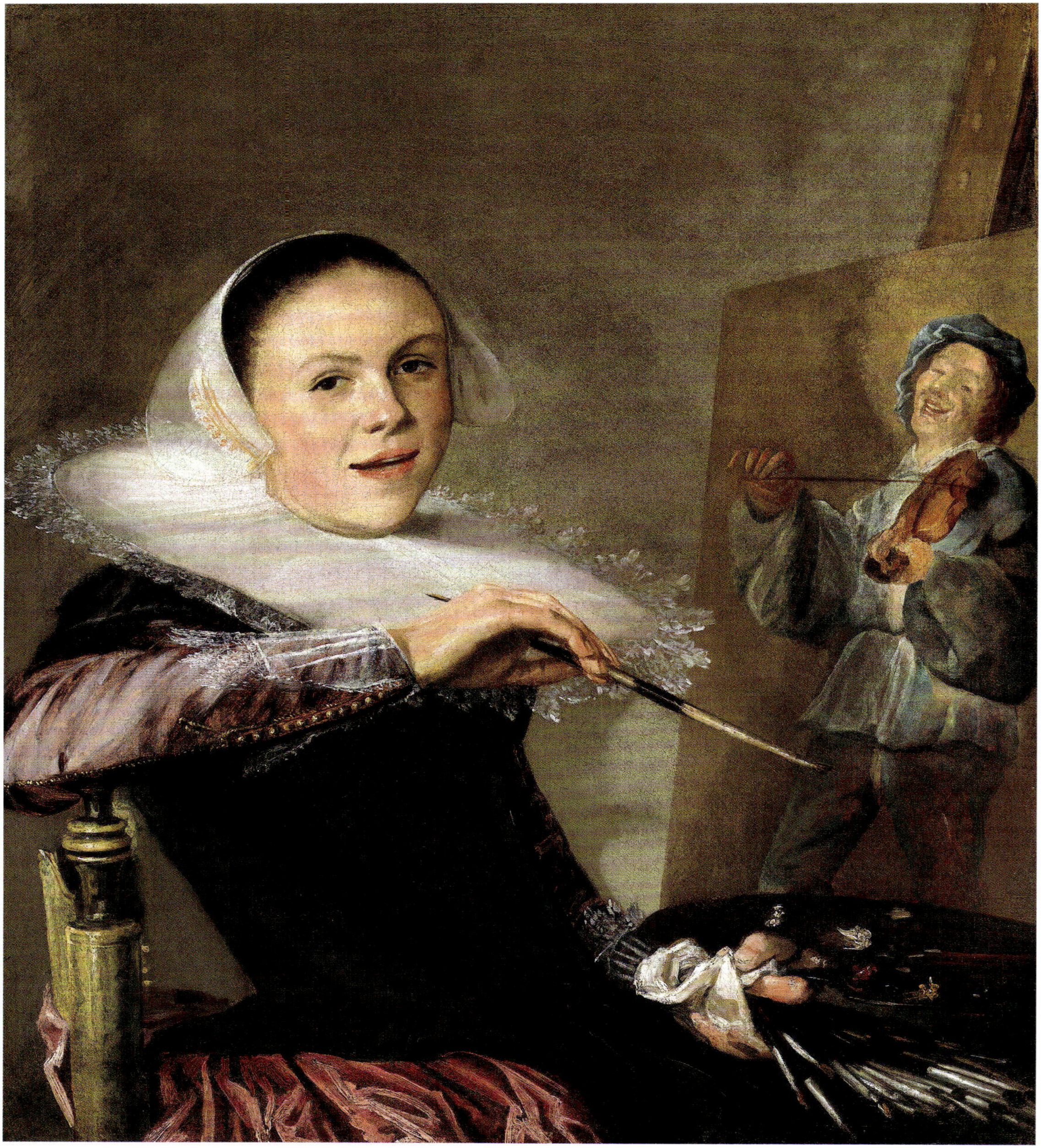

Self-portrait c.1630
Oil on canvas, 74.6 cm x 65.1 cm
National Gallery of Art, Washington

JUDITH LEYSTER (1609–60)

Self-portrait

Judith Leyster was unusual in being a successful artist at a time (known as the Golden Age) when the Dutch art world was dominated by male painters. She is believed to have been a pupil of Frans Hals since her loose, spontaneous handling of paint is comparable to his. She is also thought to have sued him for poaching one of her assistants when she was established enough to have her own workshop and students.

Leyster specialised in creating scenes of bawdiness and rowdy merrymaking that were surprising subjects for a woman artist, but very popular. Music was a specific theme in her work, with actors and dancers performing together with musicians. In her self-portrait she presents a pose that imitates the fiddler she is painting on her canvas. The two figures compliment each other. Her youthful, smiling face turns towards us, but the fiddler seems to be smiling at her. She handles her own paintbrush as if it is the bow to a violin. Yet although we see her artist's palette, she is hardly dressed for the job in hand. Her clothing is the formal costume that sitters might wear for their portraits, with pristine, carefully starched collar, cuffs and bonnet. Leyster is therefore presenting herself as artist and sitter.

She was the first woman to become a member of the painters Guild of Saint Luke in Haarlem and it is possible this painting was her offering for acceptance as her 'masterpiece'. She signed her works with her initials together with a star motif, her name meaning 'leading star'.

Though she had led an independent and successful career, she married another artist, the genre painter Molenaer, whose own popular work *The Duet* can be read as a marriage portrait. In it she plays the flute while he is seen playing a large lute. The couple had three children after which she no longer painted the scenes for which she had become so popular, instead concentrating on still lifes, which in themselves form part of the great tradition of Dutch painting.

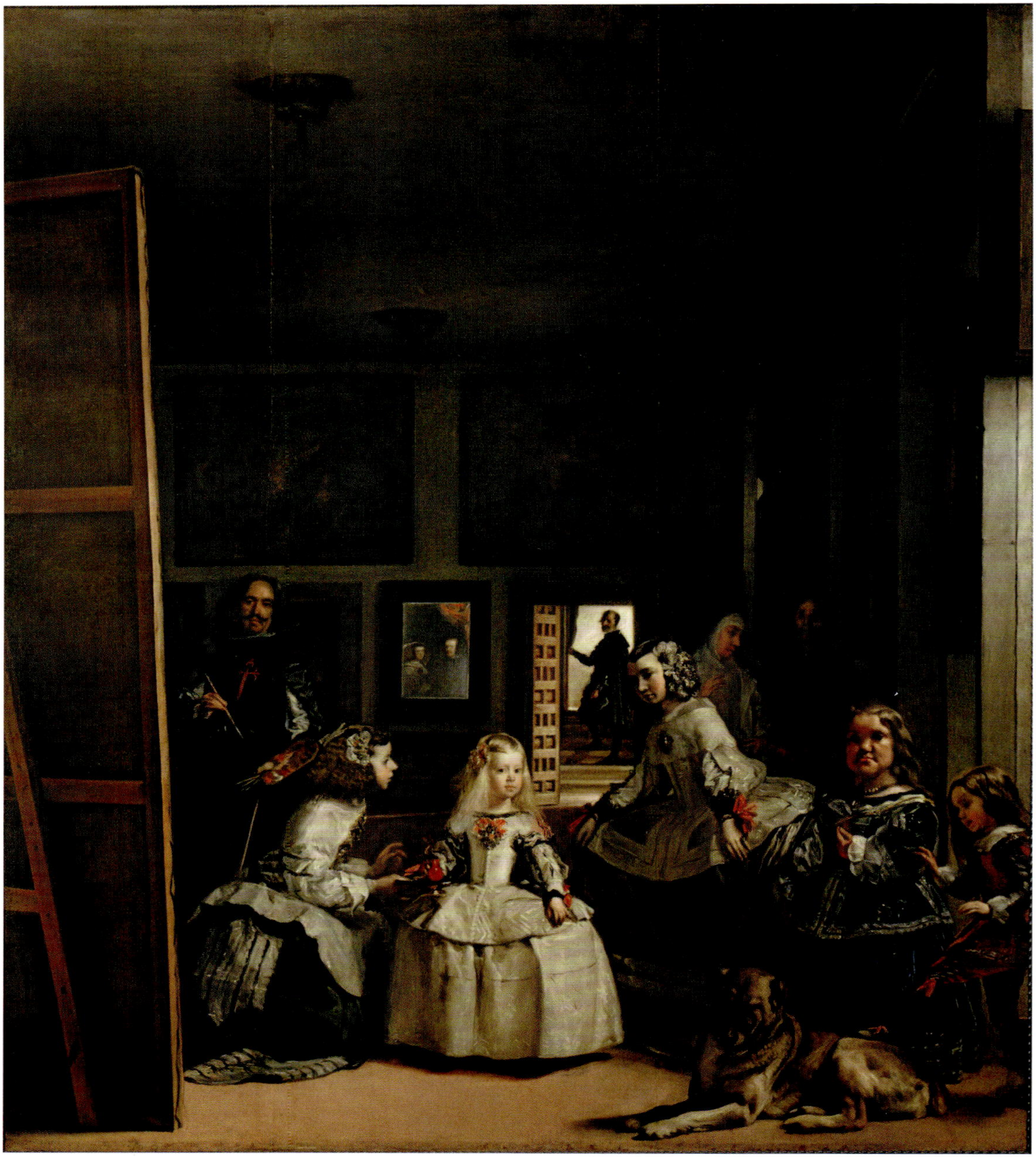

Las Meninas 1656
Oil on canvas, 320 cm x 276 cm
Museo del Prado, Madrid

DIEGO RODRÍGUEZ DE SILVA Y VELÁZQUEZ (1599–1660)

Las Meninas

As a talented child, Velázquez was already apprenticed to become an artist by the age of twelve. His rise led him to be introduced to the young Spanish King, Philip IV, when he was twenty-four. On making a successful portrait of the King, he was admitted to the royal court. Philip was greatly interested in the arts and became a keen collector. He particularly admired Rubens, who had visited Spain and met Velázquez not long after the younger painter arrived. It was in his portraiture, not only of the royal family but of many court nobles and entertainers, that Velázquez' position was secured and he worked in the court for the rest of his life.

His most celebrated painting is known as *Las Meninas* – the Maids of Honour – a title that is deceptive once closer observation of the scene is made. In the foreground is the king's daughter, the Infanta Margarita, attended by two ladies in waiting, a dwarf and a midget. Further figures, members of the royal household, stand behind them in the shadows with one standing on a distant, well-lit staircase. Velázquez himself appears, occupied in painting the huge canvas that frames the left of the picture. Hanging on the wall behind him is a portrait of the King and Queen. Or is it a mirror? If so, it might reflect the image that Velázquez is working on. Since he stares out at us, are we supposed to be the King and Queen? Or have they just entered the room, which prompts the Infanta, the dwarf, the distant courtier and the artist to acknowledge them? In this case, why does the dog lie still? Such perplexing features have encouraged many theories about the true meaning of the painting.

What is certain is that Velázquez is shown in his prestigious professional role. The painting was made some four years before he died. In 1659 he was awarded the Cross of Saint James of the Order of Santiago and it is said that Philip IV later added to the painting, marking the red cross on the artist's clothes.

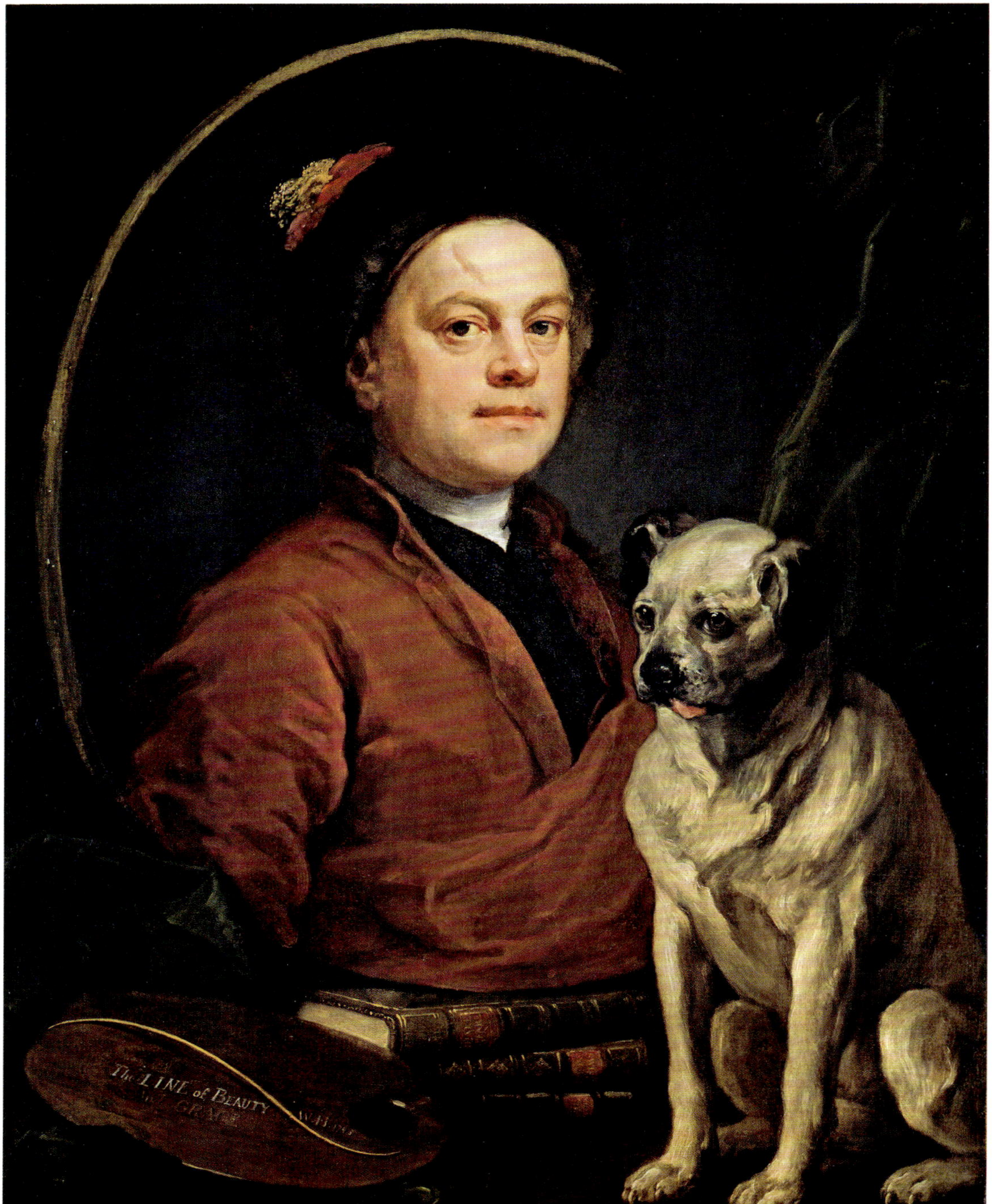
The LINE of BEAUTY

WILLIAM HOGARTH (1697–1764)

The Painter and His Pug

Hogarth was proud of being English. London was his home and here, as a child, though he knew the shame of the Fleet Prison (thanks to his father's debts) he persevered in setting up shop as an engraver at his mother's house in Long Lane. Printmaking was popular and he produced not only illustrations to written work, but also created a series of prints that contained comments on contemporary society. He became both history painter and portrait painter, but his 'modern moral subjects' reveal his great originality. He disliked the idea of British art becoming tainted by the invasion of foreign artists. He was an early founder of the charitable Foundling Hospital, and encouraged other artists such as Reynolds and Gainsborough to become involved. Exhibiting there, he was able to establish the first English public art gallery.

His bold self-portrait was the model for a later engraving. In it Hogarth drew a comparison with his dog, Trump, to emphasise his pugnacious character. Hogarth believed pugs (he had several) were particularly English. Lying next to Trump is a pile of books by Shakespeare, Milton and Swift, revealing Hogarth's admiration of English drama, poetry and satire. Their inclusion suggests he considered himself their equal. The artist's palette supports a sweeping stroke and the words 'The Line of Beauty' ('and Grace' can also be detected.) Compositions, he believed, could be enhanced if they were more simply based on elegant, serpentine lines. The motif was puzzling. 'The bait soon took,' he later wrote, 'No Egyptian Hieroglyphic ever amused more than it did for a time.'

In the form of an engraving, the painting's appearance was reversed once printed on paper and was not true to the original mirrored reflection. Hogarth wanted to keep his forehead scar in the right place, so made a slight alteration to the engraving. It is said he liked to push back his hat to show the scar, proud of this distinctive mark.

In 1753 his anti-academic book *The Analysis of Beauty* was published in which he explained his theories on beauty and grace. It was the first formal art treatise to be written in English.

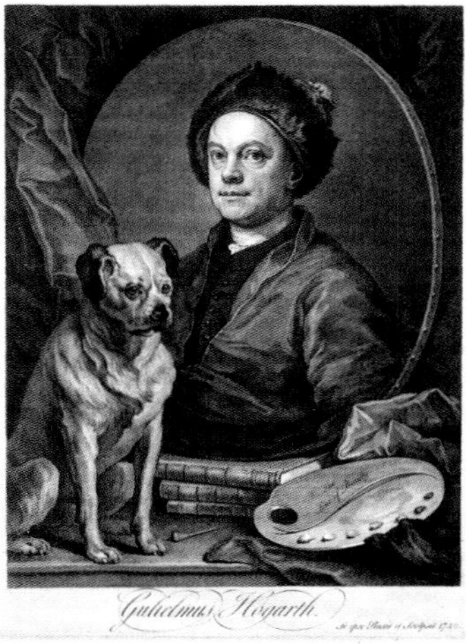

Self-portrait 1749
Engraving, 37 cm x 27 cm
Private collection

The Painter and His Pug 1745
Oil on canvas, 90 x 69.9 cm
Tate Gallery, London

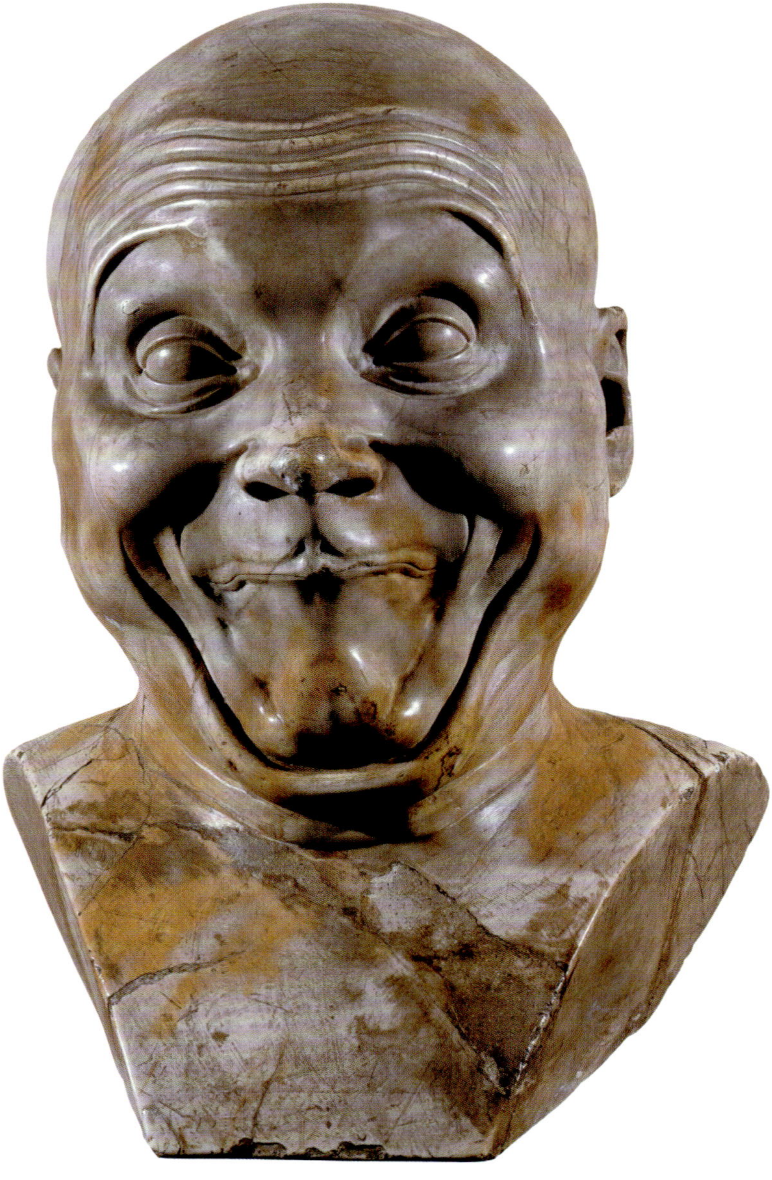

Self-portrait as a Jester from the series *Character Heads* 1770
Alabaster, height 42 cm
Österreichische Galerie Belvedere, Vienna

FRANZ XAVER MESSERSCHMIDT (1736–83)

Self-portrait as a Jester

Having been trained by two uncles who were both reputable sculptors, Messerschmidt moved forward in his own career, producing work in the Baroque style favoured by the Austrian royal court. Despite his success he took up the less flamboyant, more severe Neoclassical style, applying much he had learned from a study trip to Rome in 1769. The Romans had mastered the art of sculpted portraiture which they developed in both relief and in the round, for use especially in funerary monuments. Capturing the likeness of a face was essential to evoke an eternal image of the deceased.

Although Messerschmidt had been teaching at the Viennese Academy, his failure to gain the post of professor of sculpture, when his reputation was at its height, came as a terrible blow. This rejection was due to his suffering an illness that profoundly affected him mentally. He admitted to states of confusion, even nightly visits from demons, as well as an interest in necromancy. Away from Vienna, the city of his success, he returned to his birthplace where he began work on an extraordinary series of sculpted portraits that was to dominate his later years.

The sixty-four different heads he created display many conflicting emotions that could be associated with his suffering. Most are assumed to be self-portraits. Each one appears expressive in the extreme and he is said to have pinched himself in the rib, in order to gain the right kind of facial distortion he was seeking. His head is often bald, emphasising his features, but occasionally the neck's length is altered, or hair is added, or details are at variance within the series as a whole. But over the thirteen years he spent on them, his own appearance would have changed. Some of the titles are amusing such as *Afflicted with Constipation* or *A Hypocrite and Slanderer* which help an understanding of his intentions. Physiognomy was a popular study in the eighteenth century and Messerschmidt intended the heads should have a scientific basis. Instead they have become his own most celebrated, and amusing, contribution to the art of portrait sculpture.

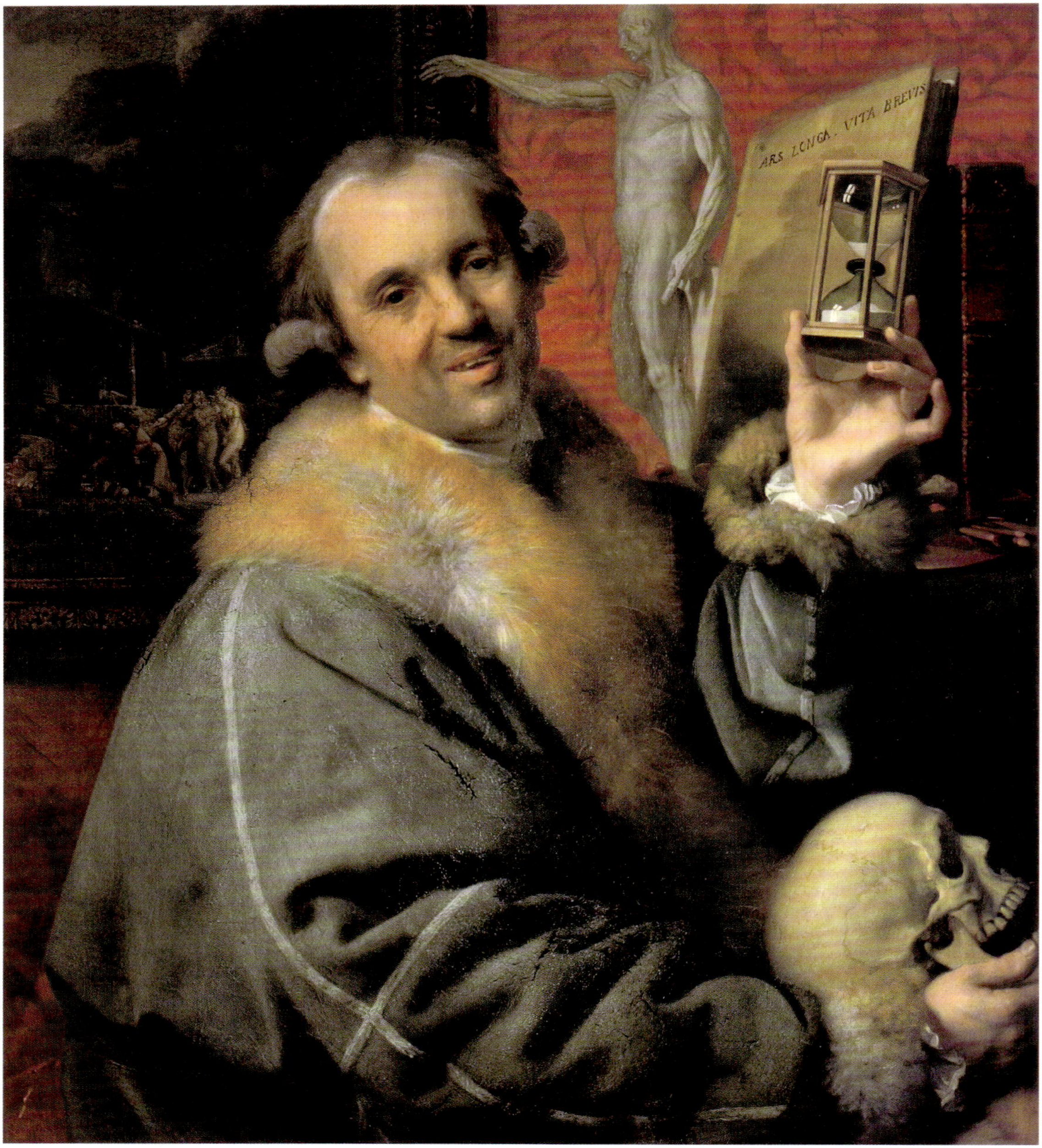

Self-portrait (with Hourglass and Skull) c.1776
Oil on panel, 87.5 cm x 77 cm
Uffizi, Florence

JOHAN ZOFFANY (1733–1810)

Self-portrait (with Hourglass and Skull)

Though he was born in Frankfurt, it was his arrival in England in 1760 that marked the beginning of Zoffany's rise to fortune as a portrait painter. His charming personality facilitated his acceptance in court and he was soon a favourite of King George III and Queen Charlotte. Not only did he paint for the aristocracy, he was also known for his popular 'conversation pieces', small, informal group portraits. He achieved further success from his paintings of the theatre at a time when this was flourishing in Britain. Actors, such as David Garrick, were portrayed by Zoffany in order to bring notice to some of their most significant performances.

The Queen, as a lover of art, asked Zoffany to paint the Tribuna, the large exhibition room of the Uffizi in Florence. In the result his observation of the gallery's connoisseurs and amateurs of art contained ironic undertones that lost him royal favour. Hogarth, whom he admired, had also employed satire to make his personal social comments. To include suggestive details, adding meaning to a painting, was more than a conceit when it came to the many self-portraits Zoffany made. In observing himself, he also commented on human nature.

The Uffizi held a unique collection of self-portraits begun by Leopoldo di Medici in 1664. Zoffany hoped to be included and his own contribution is still there. It shows him smiling and successful, dressed in fabulous fur, surrounded by what first appears to be conventional artistic attributes. There is a painting on the wall that contains the classical figures of the Three Graces. A cast of the famous skinned figure by Houdon, which was used for studying the body, is also there. But Zoffany is making a further point than to simply acknowledge his own profession. He comments on the profession itself. In one hand he holds an hourglass, symbol of time passing. In the other he holds a brilliantly painted lifelike human skull. Why should he smile while holding such portentious objects? On the upright book behind him is written the words 'Ars Longa Vita Brevis' explaining that though life is short, art lasts for ever.

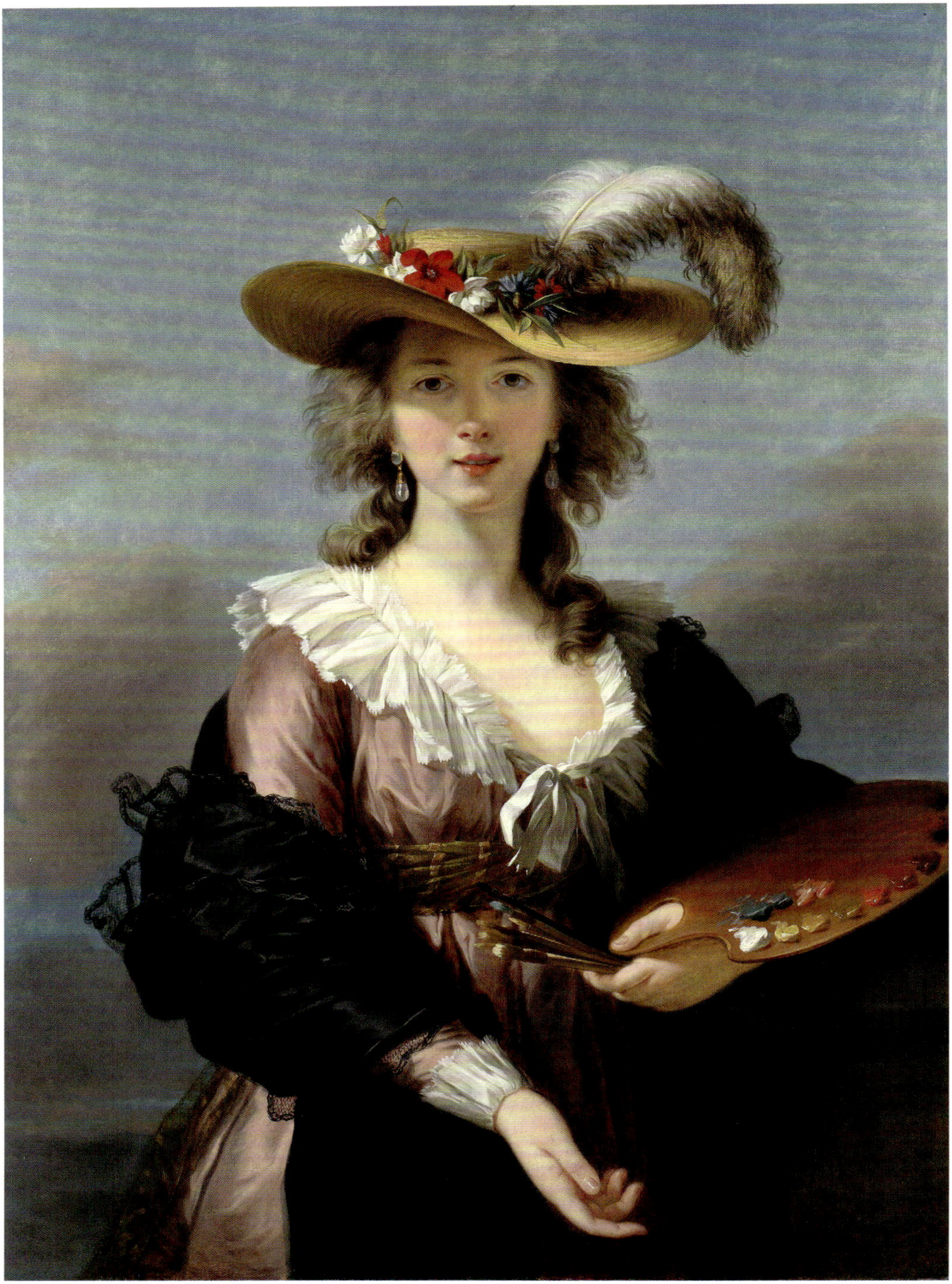

ELISABETH VIGÉE LE BRUN

(1755–1842)

Self-portrait in a Straw Hat

As a personal friend of Queen Marie Antoinette, the painter Elisabeth Vigée Le Brun was in a fortunate position to become one of France's most popular portrait painters. Women had not always been allowed entrance to the French Royal Academy and in 1706 they were banned. By the time she was working, this prohibition was lifted. Her flattering portrayal of prominent aristocrats led to her receiving hundreds of commissions including over twenty of the Queen.

Whilst visiting European galleries, she came across the painting *Le Chapeau de Paille* (The Straw Hat) by Rubens. 'Perhaps one must be a painter in order to appreciate all the power here displayed by Rubens,' she recalled and went on to describe her admiration for the delicate lighting he used: 'This painting inspired me to the point where I made my own portrait in search of the same effect.' She placed herself in a similarly open-air, sunlit location, where delicate clouds pass behind her. Although Rubens' work did not contain a straw hat, she painted a simple one for herself placing on it fresh flowers and a decorative plume. Despite the formal earrings she wears, her pert and pretty face is surrounded by surprisingly unkempt hair. In some of her paintings of the Queen she had been criticised for the natural look she had given the monarch. But the concept of rural simplicity appealed to both of them.'I detested the female style of dress then in fashion,' she said, 'I bent all my efforts upon rendering it a little more picturesque.' She wears loosely hung clothes, à la grecque, without restrictive stiff corsetry, further enhancing the emphasis on her femininity. She holds her artist's materials, symbol of her work, but like many of her portraits, this self-image is entirely idealised.

At the dawn of the French Revolution, owing to her closeness to the Queen (whom she defended always) Vigée Le Brun fled to Europe in secret with her daughter. She returned in 1814 and as an elderly woman in her eighties, wrote her revealing memoirs.

Self-portrait in a Straw Hat 1782
Oil on canvas, 97.8 cm x 70.5 cm
National Gallery, London

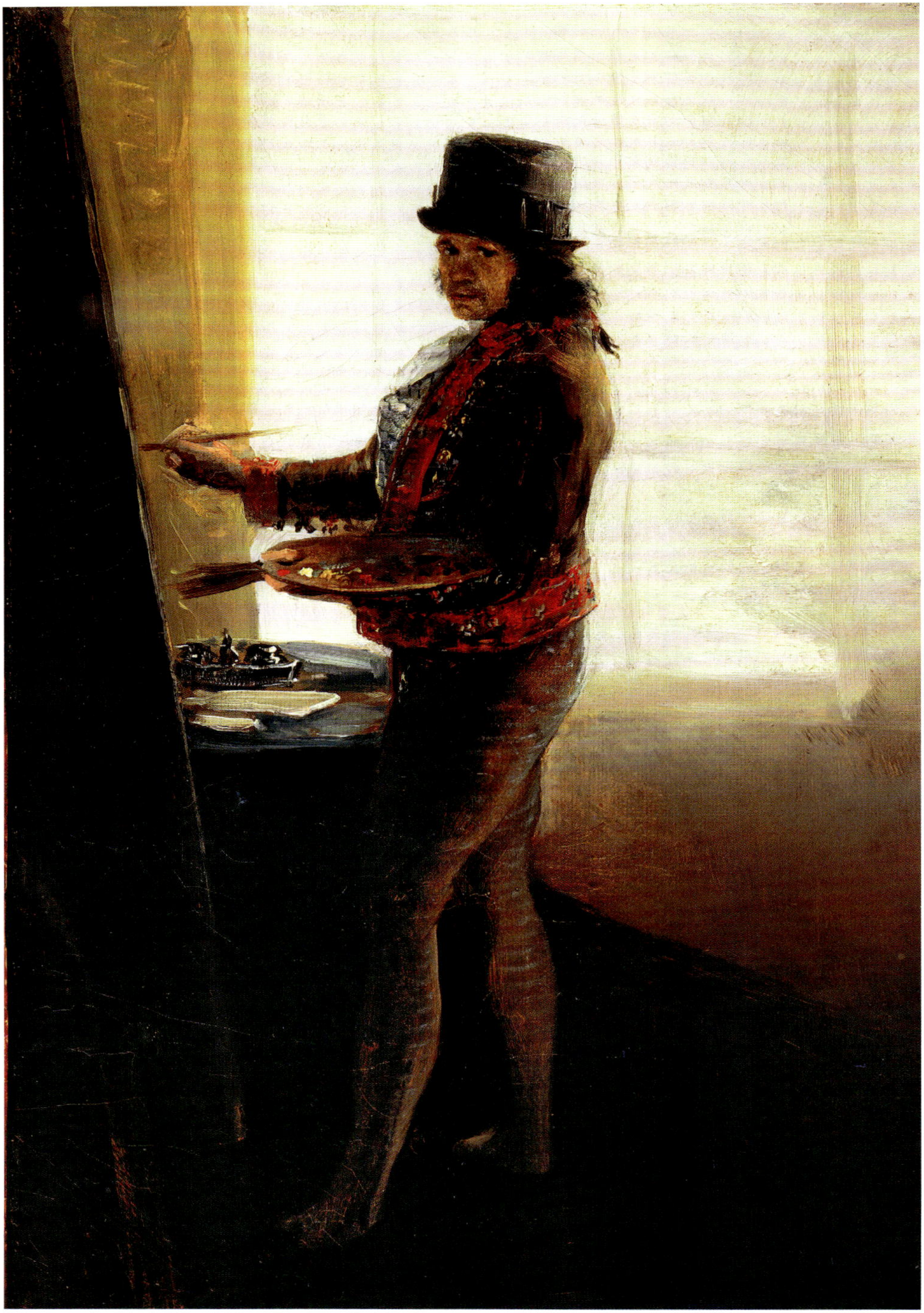

FRANCISCO DE GOYA (1746–1828)

Self-portrait in the Studio

Full-length self-portraits are less common than the half-length, and required a very large mirror placed at a distance to accommodate the reflection of the entire body. Goya's self-portrait is nothing like the size of the large canvas he is seen to be facing in the painting. Much of the image, therefore, is invention. He stands securely in the central space, confident in his stance, holding a sizeable palette and brushes as he prepares his next stroke. He looks out at himself (his features recognisable from other self-portraits) in a single moment in time. Yet he is starkly silhouetted against the dazzling light of his studio window. This light would, in reality, flash and rebound from a mirror, disturbing his vision. The angle of the window and even the position of the canvas are at variance with logical reality. Is the light that surrounds him indicative of the light of the artist's inspiration?

Goya deliberately identifies himself with Spain as he is seen wearing the traditional costume of a *majo*. His almost comic hat bears small candles – he liked to finish his paintings at night. Though it is day-time here, this added source of light might be a reference to the artist's own powers of perception.

As a portrait painter in the royal court, Goya was expected to flatter his sitters. Yet in his private world he revealed many growing personal fears. 'I wish people would leave me alone and let me live quietly,' he wrote, 'carrying out the work which I am obliged to do and spending the remaining time on things of my own.' Only two years after this self-portrait was made he became ill and suffered total deafness that lasted all his life. The isolation this imposed on him did not hinder the progress of his increasingly imaginative work. His etchings reveal his despondancy over contemporary Spanish society and his horror of the state of war. The paintings from the walls of his own house are dark and menacing. Eventually he died in exile in France. Much of his career, like so many of his Romantic contemporaries, had been spent expressing deep concern over universal issues.

Self Portrait in the Studio 1791
Oil on canvas, 42 x 28 cm
Academia San Fernando, Madrid

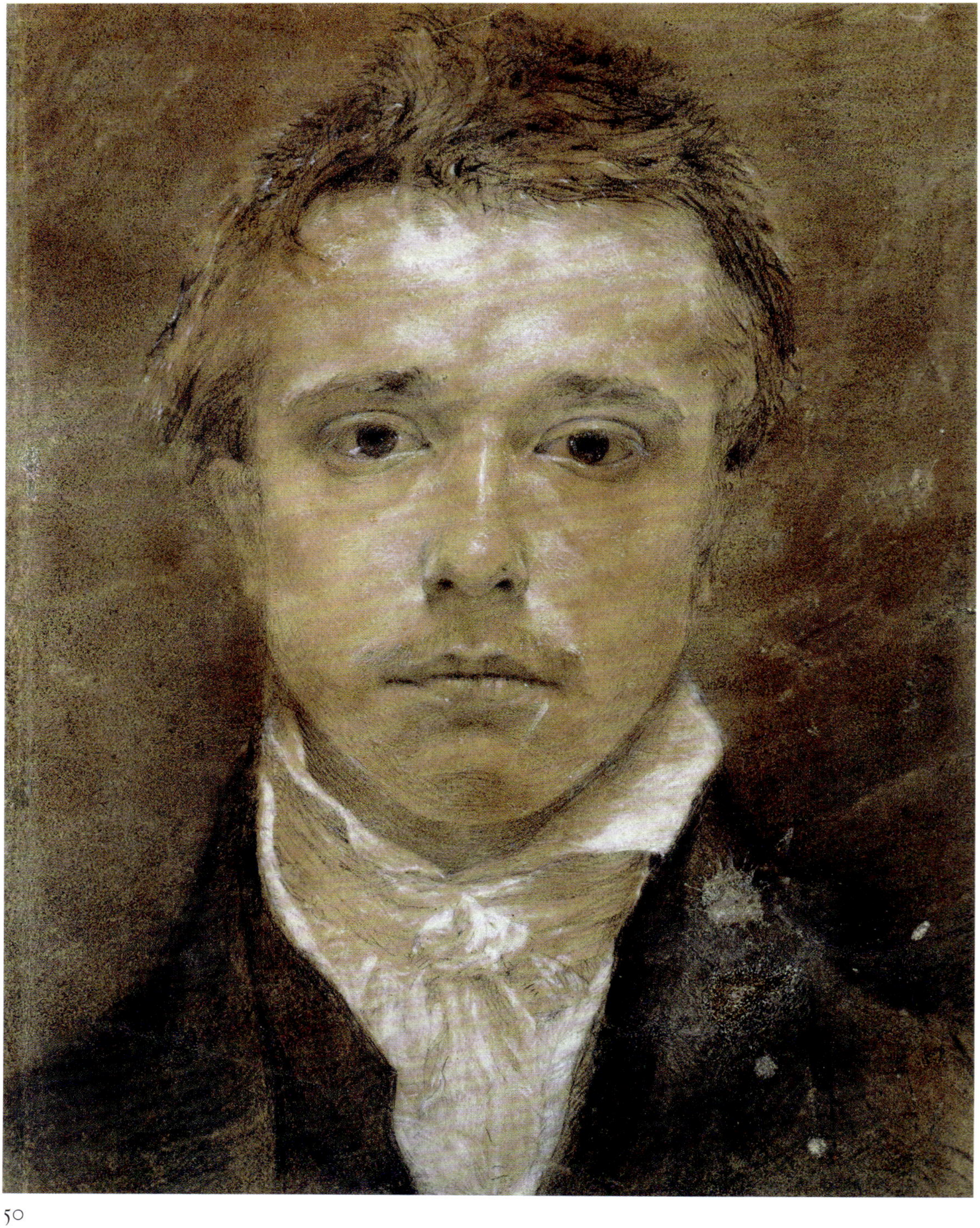

SAMUEL PALMER (1805–81)

Self-portrait

Palmer decided to become an artist at the age of thirteen and trained with a private tutor who advised him to study nature. When he was fourteen he exhibited at the Royal Academy and was soon to meet other artists in London, including William Blake, who encouraged him away from current trends. His work became less topographical, more visionary, revealing nature as a spiritual source, a concept explored by the Romantic poets. Together with a group of fellow artists, Palmer formed a brotherhood known as the Ancients, who revelled in the countryside of Shoreham, Kent, where he lived for nearly ten years. By using sepia, a dark liquid made from cuttlefish, and mixing this with gum, he created a medium that resembled textured printmaking. It was highly suitable for rural scenes of dense woodland or luxuriant fields touched by magical moonlight. He also used pencil, pen and inks, watercolour and gouache as he explored ways to evoke the pastoral life of England that he feared would soon disappear in the industrial age.

The young man, slightly dishevelled, seen in daring frontal close-up is the image of a Romantic artist. Palmer had hardly begun his career when he drew this striking self-portrait in a medium that lent itself to a dramatic monochrome colouring. White chalk picks up the nuances of his forehead and nasal area, his delicate lashes and the bright folds of his shirt and cravate as if he is illumined from an unseen source above. His dark eyes stare with an impenetrable gaze, as he submits to deep reflection. Palmer kept the drawing all his life. It was inherited by his son who wrote on the back 'Samuel Palmer by himself. His mouth was difficult to draw, sensitive and full of expression and feeling.'

Turner had painted himself earlier in a similar way, in dark tones, staring out of the canvas, a young man with his future ahead of him. Both artists were to become two of the most significant painters of landscape in the history of British art.

Self-portrait c.1826
Chalk on paper, 29 cm x 22.9 cm
Ashmolean Museum, University of Oxford

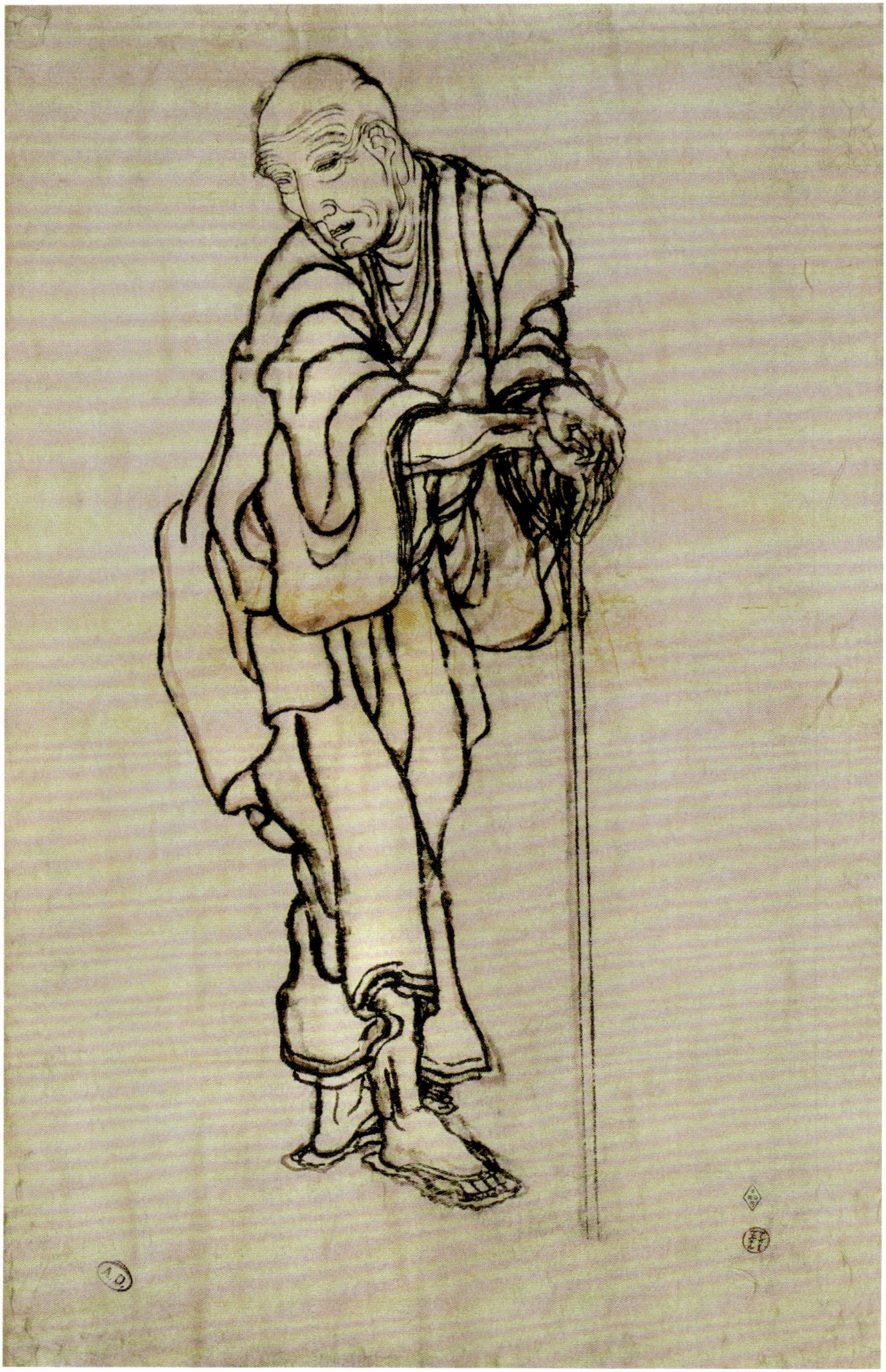

KATSUSHIKA HOKUSAI (1760–1849)

Self-portrait as an Old Man

For nearly two hundred years, Japan was prohibited from trading with the west. By the mid-1850s, these restrictive internal laws were lifted and as commercial links grew, so the recent art of Japan was discovered. Prints that were used as packaging were found to be of artistic merit. In Paris, the craze for collecting saw the opening of shops selling Japanese goods. 'Japonisme' fired the imagination of many artists. At his home in Giverny, Monet owned a collection of over two hundred Japanese prints that remain there today.

One of the most inventive artists discovered by the west was Hokusai. His series, *Thirty-Six Views of Mount Fuji*, showing the volcano seen from unusual viewpoints, brought him recognition firstly in his home country and later worldwide. The famous image of *The Great Wave Off Kanagawa* reveals Mount Fuji far on the distant horizon, beneath the wave. Such unusual means of representing the world encouraged western artists to rethink conventional methods. Flat areas of colour with no reference to light and shade, strong outlines, sharp angles of perspective that the Japanese had used in printmaking were now incorporated into modern paintings.

Hokusai had many pupils throughout his career and created various illustrated manuals including his book of *manga*, popular figures from everyday life. His most significant work was done late in his life. The figure of an old man, considered to be a self-portrait, is done entirely in assured, clear lines. Each fold of his clothing falls distinctly from the others that drape his twisting body. Detail is given to his sandalled feet and the hands that clasp his long walking stick. The face is not unlike the mask of an actor, such characters being popular in Japanese culture and illustration.

'At seventy-three, I began to grasp the structures of birds and beasts, insects and fish, and of the way plants grow,' Hokusai said. 'If I go on trying, I will surely understand them still better by the time I am eighty-six, so that by ninety I will have penetrated to their essential nature. At one hundred, I may well have a positively divine understanding of them.'

Self-portrait as an Old Man c.1830
Ink on paper, 37 x 23.5 cm
Bibliothèque des Arts Décoratifs, Paris

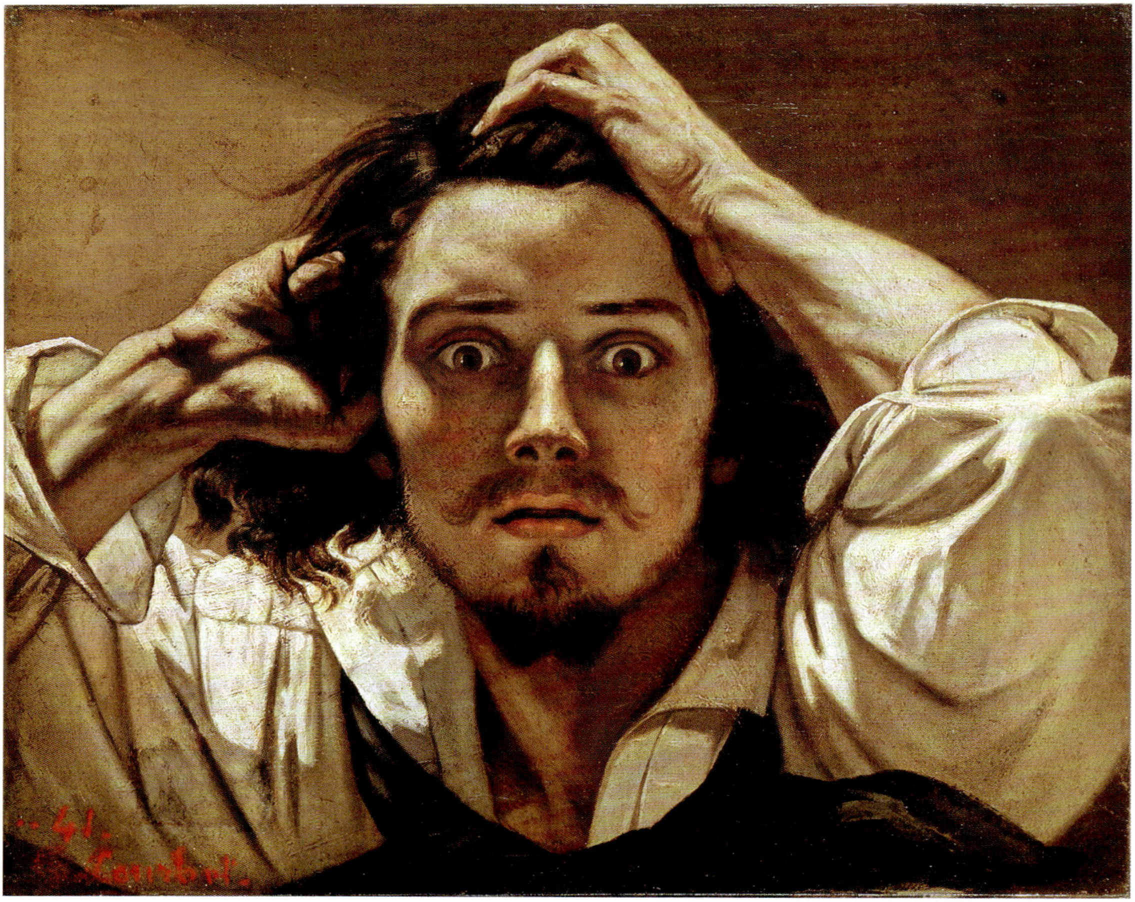

The Desperate Man (Self-portrait) 1841
Oil on canvas, 45 x 54 cm
Private collection

GUSTAVE COURBET (1819–77)

The Desperate Man (Self-portrait)

Of several self-portraits Courbet made, this 'desperate man' appears to be the image of a frustrated, enraged artist on the brink of madness. Others show him with a black dog (the two resembling each other), as a cellist, as a wounded man and in a huge canvas he described as a 'real allegory'. Here he is in his studio surrounded by a naked model, a cat, a peasant boy and people from the worlds of politics and the arts. He painted himself not so much in different guises, but at periods when he questioned his artistic identity. One tiny portrait shows him addressing the Mediterranean. 'The sea's voice is tremendous,' he explained, 'but not loud enough to drown the voice of Fame, crying my name to the entire world.'

Courbet was born near Besançon in the Jura in the small town of Ornans. His early paintings were not pleasant, rural views of its remarkable landscape, but revealed the harshness of peasant life there. He was concerned with depicting real events with a stark, pictorial honesty. Similarly, he rejected dishonesty when it came to portraits. He was not afraid to show the female nude as unidealised, plump or even with mud on her feet. He claimed he could not paint an angel as he had never seen one. Included in the paintings of the natural woodland and cliffs near Ornans are brutal scenes of the hunt that suggest his critical view of society. His political activities led to his imprisonment. A self-portrait made afterwards shows him deep in thought at the prison window.

The 'desperate man' may have had specific sources that separate it from the notion of the Romantic artist. Rembrandt had done many self-portraits, including engravings showing him wide-eyed, staring and with different, alarming expressions. In 1851 Courbet was described as a 'socialist painter' to which he replied 'I am first and foremost a realist.' Is this a realistic view of him? Though his public persona was a lively extrovert, he once wrote to a friend, 'Behind the laughing mask that you see I conceal inside me suffering, bitterness and a sadness that clings to my heart like a vampire.'

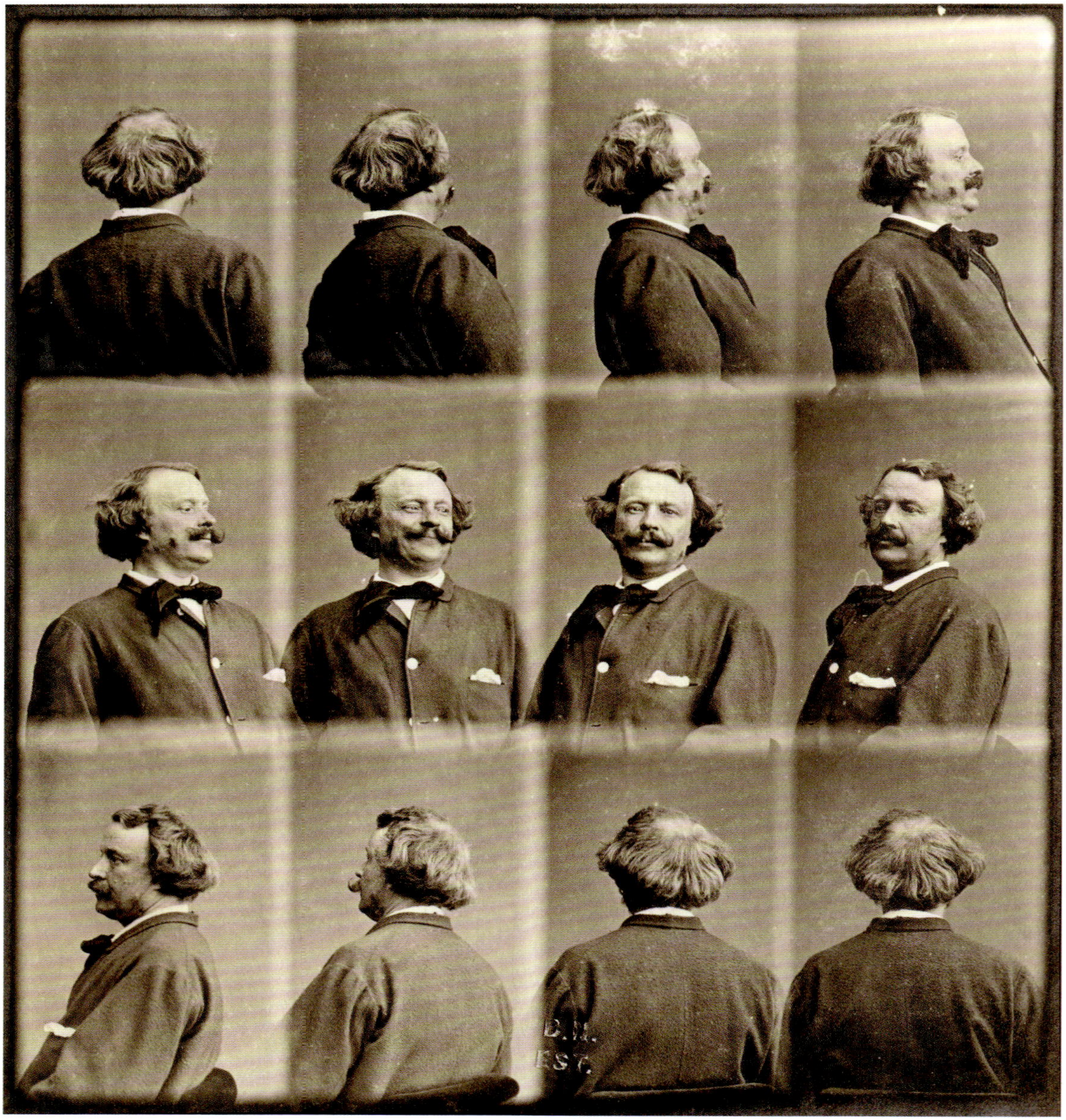

Revolving Self-portrait 1865
Sheet of 12 photographs, gelatin si ver print
Bibliothéque Nationale de France, Paris

NADAR (GASPARD-FÉLIX TOURNACHON) (1820–1910)

Revolving Self-portrait

The name Nadar was a play on the artist's true surname, changing Tournachon to *tourne à dard* meaning, 'one who stings'. This was in keeping with Nadar's skills as a caricaturist during his early career when he worked for several Parisian journals. By the 1860s he gave up the profession having gained a reputation in photography. At first he took pictures of his friends which led on to portraits of some of the great politicians and artists of his day. He explored ways of presenting his sitters naturally, rejecting conventional studio devices that contributed to an artificiality, unrelated to their personalities. Instead of using painted backdrops, accessories and retouching techniques, he examined how relaxed poses and the effects of different lighting might reveal his subjects' true characters. He was a pioneer of the use of artifical light in photography, experimenting in the catacombs and sewers of underground Paris.

The twelve photographs of himself are seen as revolving since they show him from all angles. When placed in sequence and set to motion, it is as if he is turning in a circle in front of the camera. In one of the frames he suppresses a wide smile while the next shows him to be more serious.

Nadar was the first person to take aerial photographs. This was thanks to his passion for ballooning. In 1863 he had built his own large balloon, Le Géant, and his enthusiasm encouraged his friend Jules Verne to include the activity in his novels. Another self-portrait shows Nadar sitting in the basket of a balloon with his wife. The evident studio set-up (with an enlarged photo of a mountainous valley behind them) does not mean he was reluctant to explore the reality of air-travel. He became President of the Society for the Encouragement of Aerial Locomotion by Means of Heavier than Air Machines. Verne was the society's secretary.

For years he rented out his studio at 25 Boulevard des Capucines to artists and intellectuals for meetings and exhibitions. In 1874 the group of artists who would become known as the Impressionists had their first exhibition there.

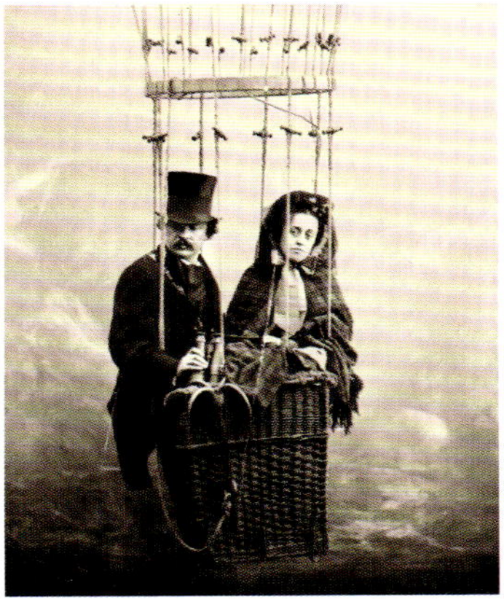

Self-portrait with Ernestine in a Balloon Gondola c.1865
Gelatin silver print, sheet 8.6 x 7.7 cm
National Gallery of Art, Washington

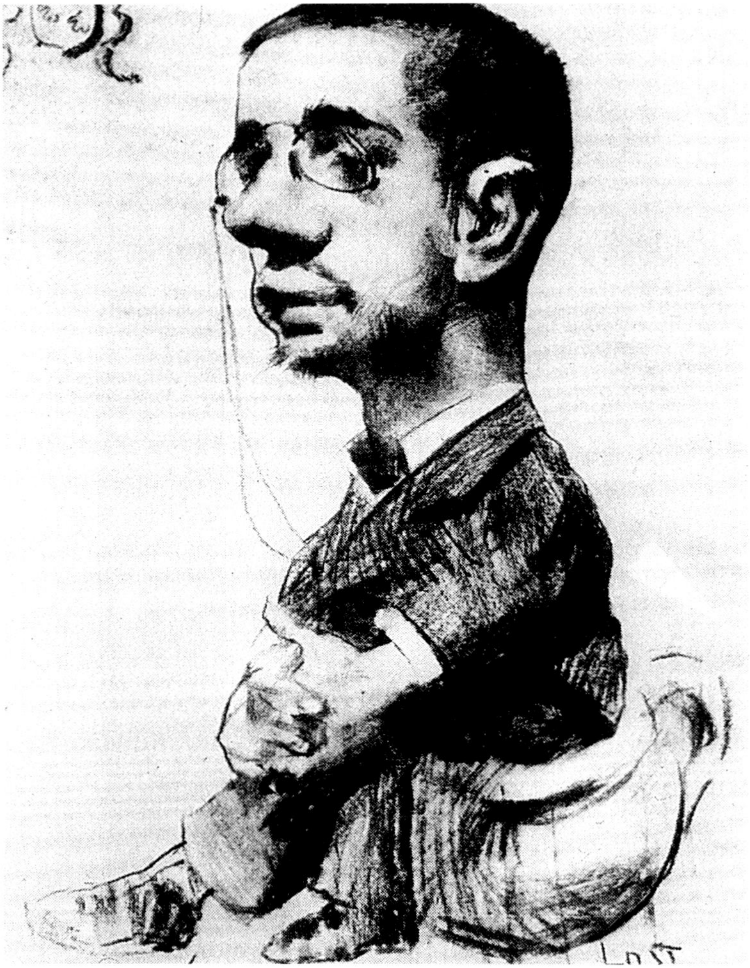

Self-caricature 'Lost' 1882
Charcoal on paper
Maison Natale de Toulouse-Lautrec, Albi

HENRI DE TOULOUSE-LAUTREC (1864–1901)

Self-caricature 'Lost'

For much of his life, Toulouse-Lautrec searched for ways of alleviating the suffering he experienced, the result of physical deformities he had known since birth. As a child he felt unusual pain in his legs and broke first one leg then the other in minor falls. His mother embarked on a series of primitive cures for him that could never work. By the time he was an adult his upper body appeared normal, but he was unnaturally short.

He grew up in the Languedoc where his aristocratic family owned both a large townhouse in Albi, as well as a fine, old country château. The young Lautrec was in possession of a good sense of humour and was popular with visitors. From an early age, as a pastime, he loved to draw and often portrayed family members. As they knew he would be financially secure, his parents did not dissuade him from artistic ambitions, especially if these amused him. He had an eye for characterisation combined with humour that reflected not only the people with whom he chose to socialise, but also his own outlook on his contemporaries.

Inside one of his many childhood sketchbooks, he drew a self-portrait that shows his ability to capture truth through caricature. His large head with his round nose (that frequently dripped) is held upright, almost haughtily, above his diminished body that sits comfortably on an outsized chamberpot. Relaxed, he clasps his hands round his crossed knees. He may be a figure of laughter, but he is quite at ease with himself. Inscribed near the drawing is the word 'Lost' – a bilingual reference to 'Toulouse'. At the time his father was concerned about the prestigious family name that could be traced back to early medieval history. The child Lautrec had practised several alternative titles including 'Monsieur le Vicomte', a name he one day was due to inherit.

Despite medical warnings, Lautrec spiced his love of life with alcohol and he died young. The writer Jules Renard said of him, 'The more you see of him, the bigger he gets.'

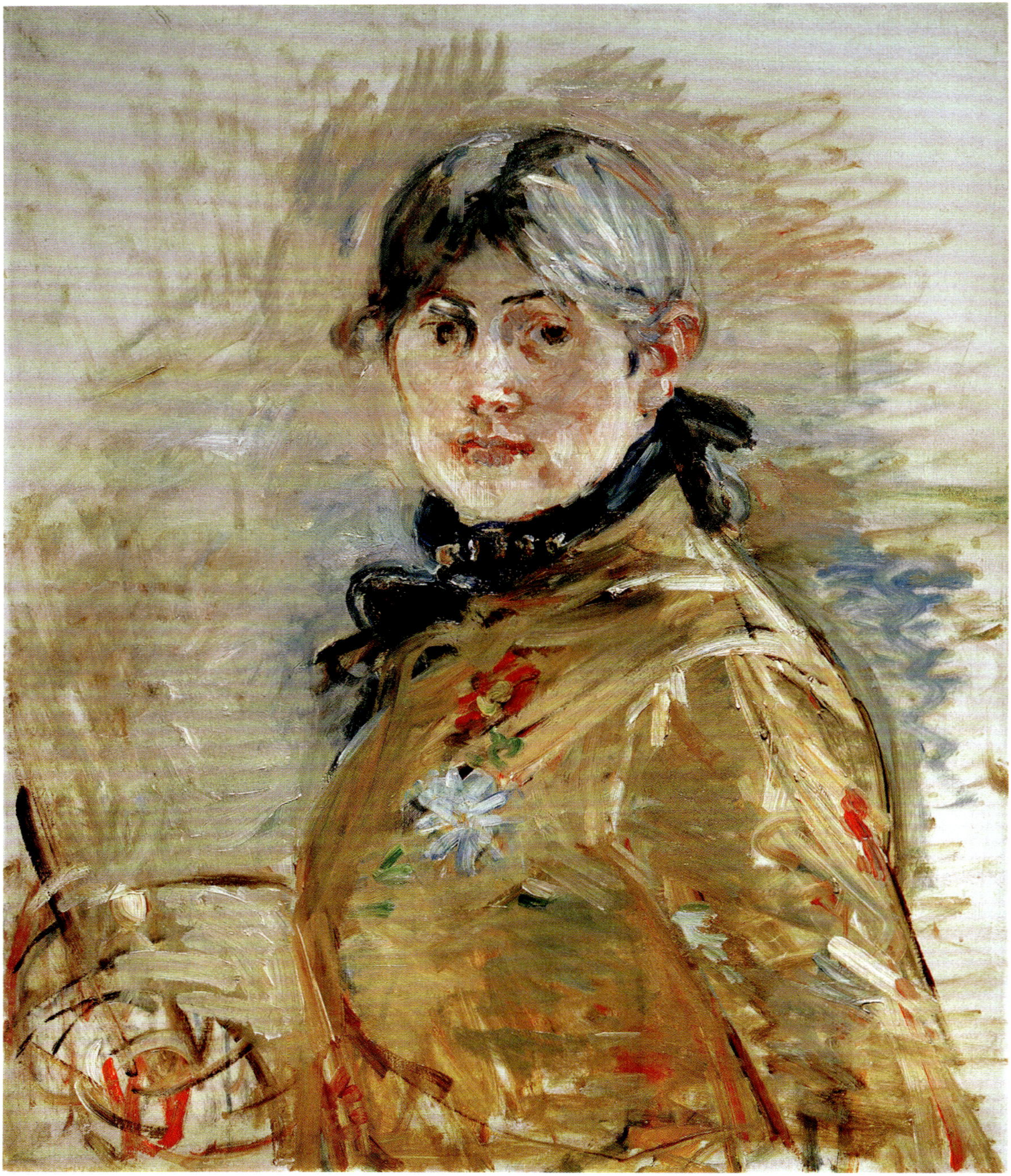

BERTHE MORISOT (1841–95)

Self-portrait

As young women, Berthe Morisot and her sister were encouraged to take up painting by their parents. Their family was said to be related to the great French artist, Fragonard. Following some early training, the girls registered at the Louvre as copyists, allowing them to study art in the great museum's collection. Berthe was introduced to the landscape artist Corot who encouraged her to paint ouside, *en plein air*. Working in Normandy, as well as on the outskirts of Paris, she began to create paintings that were accepted for showing at the Salon, the official exhibition area that allowed artists to achieve a certain status.

In 1868 Berthe met Edouard Manet who was already an established painter and who had, in recent years, become notorious. The two became close friends and regarded each other's work with interest, exchanging ideas. Whilst Manet still preferred to submit works for the Salon, by 1874, together with other like-minded artists, Berthe sought an alternative place to exhibit and the photographer Nadar lent them his studio in the centre of Paris. The group known as Impressionists was established, the name being a derogatory term to describe their handling of paint. Berthe decided never to show at the Salon again, and continued to exhibit with the Impressionists at each of their exhibitions except for one, following the birth of her daughter, Julie. She had married Manet's brother and her subject matter revolved round her own social life, particularly Julie's growing years.

'My ambition is limited to capturing something transient,' she said. Her painting has been described as 'feminine', probably because of her light brush-strokes, her depiction of domestic scenes and the fact that she had success while working among men. She wrote at length of her commitment to her work as well as her methods. 'It is important to express oneself,' she explained, 'provided the feelings are real and are taken from your own experience.' Berthe's self-portrait shows a fresh, lively approach to her work, characteristic of the Impressionists' spontaneity. 'Real painters understand with a brush in their hand,' she said.

Self-portrait 1885
Oil on canvas, 61 x 50 cm
Musée Marmottan, Paris

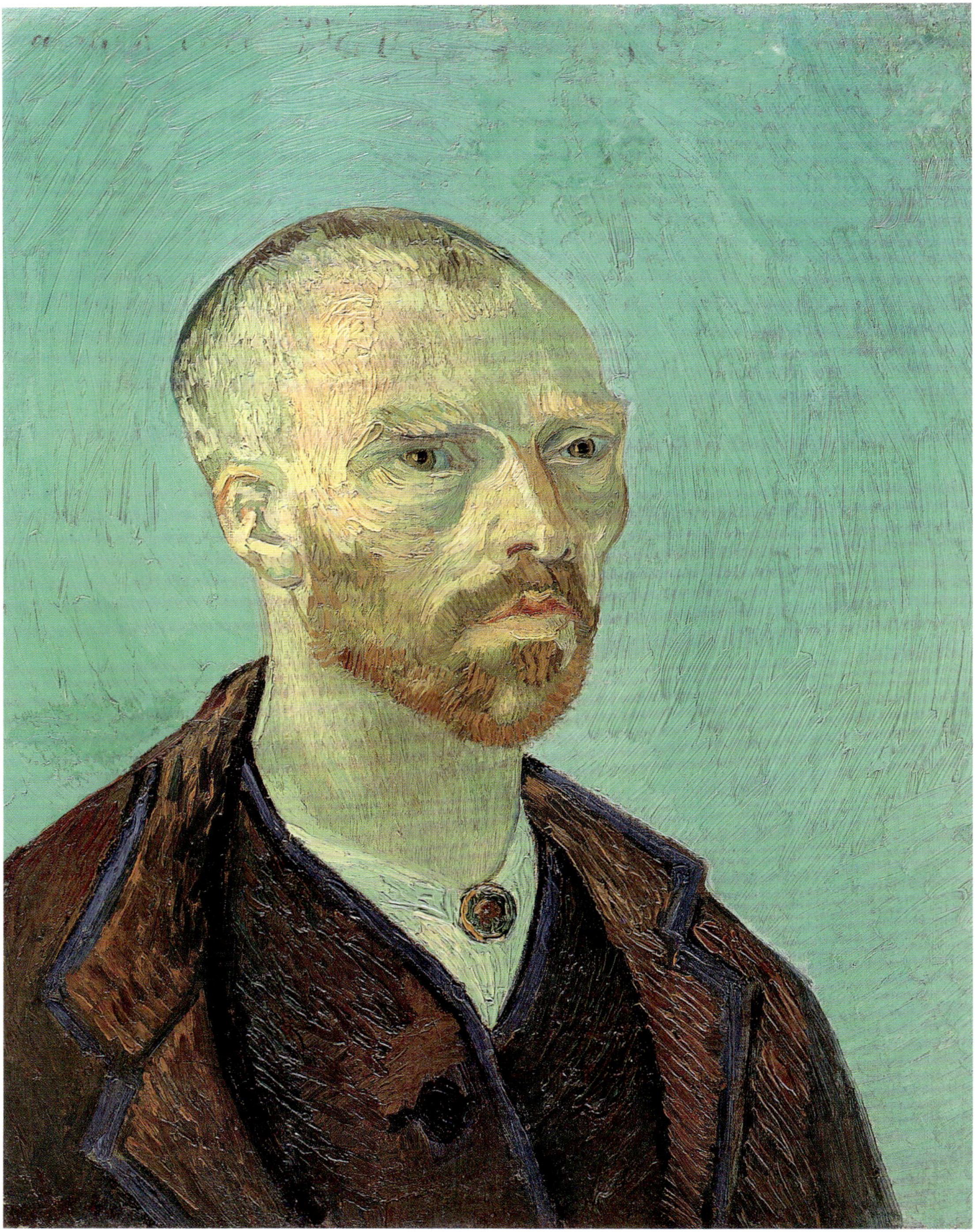

VINCENT VAN GOGH (1853–90)

Self-portrait for Gauguin

As a young man, Van Gogh hoped to become a priest, following his father who was a Protestant minister. He did not succeed. Turning towards art, he claimed, 'It is the same with evangelists as it is with artists.' His early career led him to depict the impoverished lives of peasants in the Borinage area of Belgium. His brother Theo worked for an art dealer in Paris and it was here that Van Gogh was introduced to the work of the Impressionists. His palette lightened and from then on he preferred to use bright colours. In Paris he discovered how Japanese printmakers had illustrated the world and he was determined to capture that vision in his own work. Travelling south, he settled in Provence which he felt had some resemblance to Japanese landscapes. There he hoped to found a community of like-minded artists. He encouraged a few friends to join him in Arles and suggested beforehand that they exchanged self-portraits.

Van Gogh wrote about the stark image he made of himself for Gauguin, whom he revered as a prospective master. He described the 'ashen colour – which results from the mixture of emerald green with orange lead – on a pale green background, all in harmony with the reddish brown clothing. But exaggerating my own personality as well, I instead looked for the character of a bonze, a simple worshipper of the eternal Buddha. It caused me enough pain.' To live a monastic life as artists was his ideal.

The few months Van Gogh shared with Gauguin in the south were inventive yet destructive. Applying themselves to serious work, they witnessed each other's methods. Both were strong personalities. Van Gogh, however, became increasingly emotionally unstable and having attacked his friend, he was roused enough to mutilate himself, cutting off part of one ear. Gauguin returned to Paris at once while Van Gogh was treated for his wound and later admitted to an asylum where he created some of his finest work.

In a self-portrait showing his bandaged ear, he included behind him a Japanese print revealing his continuing respect for the art of that country and an empty canvas, promise of work to come. The following year he shot himself and died.

Self-portrait for Gauguin 1888
Oil on canvas, 61 x 50 cm
Fogg Art Museum, Cambridge, Massachusetts

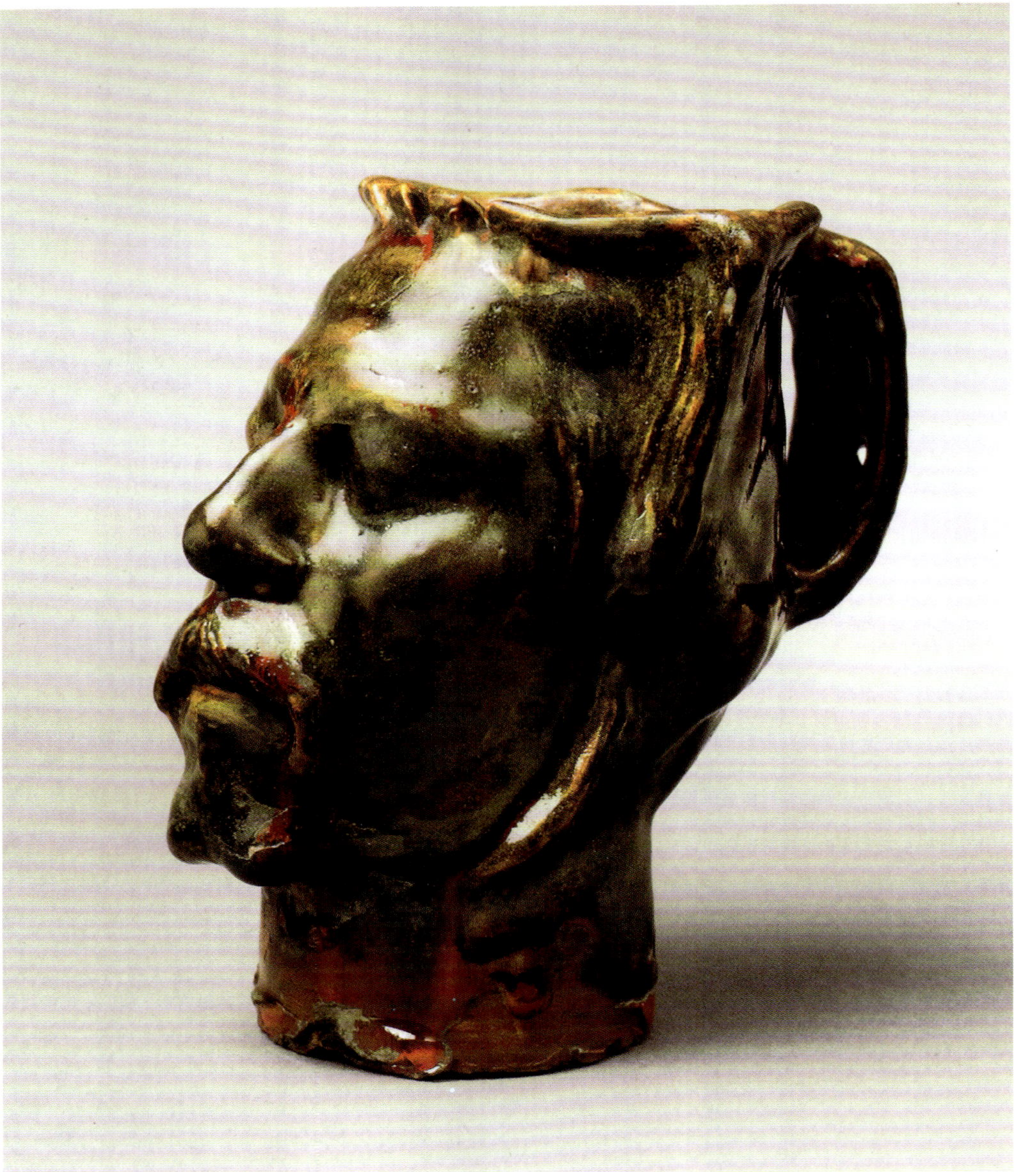

Self-portrait Vase in the Form of a Severed Head 1889
Glazed stoneware, height 19.5 cm
Danish Museum of Art and Design, Copenhagen

PAUL GAUGUIN (1848–1903)

Self-portrait Vase in the Form of a Severed Head

Gauguin was proud of his ancestry, claiming to be 'a savage', thanks to the Peruvian relatives he had on his mother's side. When he portrayed himself, he frequently included a brutal or shocking note in the work. He saw himself as a defeated and lonely Christ, as the fugitive hero of *Les Misérables*, as a lascivious seducer and as an Indian warrior. He was familiar with Peruvian pots cast as heads that had belonged to his mother and were given to his guardian, a collector of art. His interest in three-dimensional forms in wood or stone ran alongside his early efforts to become a recognised painter. His attempts at marble sculpture led him to create portrait busts of his wife and child. But it was not until 1886, when he met the professional ceramicist Ernest Chaplet, that he was able to seriously consider his own production of pottery.

In this ceramic jug, his ear-less head appears to be decapitated. His eyes are closed, his lips are slightly apart and blood appears to fall over his damp hair and moustache. Only some weeks earlier, Gauguin had witnessed the execution of a convicted murderer by public guillotine in Paris. The case had fascinated both him and his friend, Van Gogh. But it was also recently, whilst they were staying together in Provence that Van Gogh had attempted to attack Gauguin with a knife, before turning on himself. Gauguin found him in his room, his head covered with blood, his ear mutilated. He soon returned to the capital.

Why did Gauguin portray himself like this? Did he consider himself a martyr, the artist suffering for his art? Was he comparing himself not to Christ, but to John the Baptist? Or did he link his artistry to the decapitated Greek musician, Orpheus? Gauguin certainly saw himself here as a victim, though the jug soon reappeared in a painting as a simple object placed on a table filled with decorative flowers.

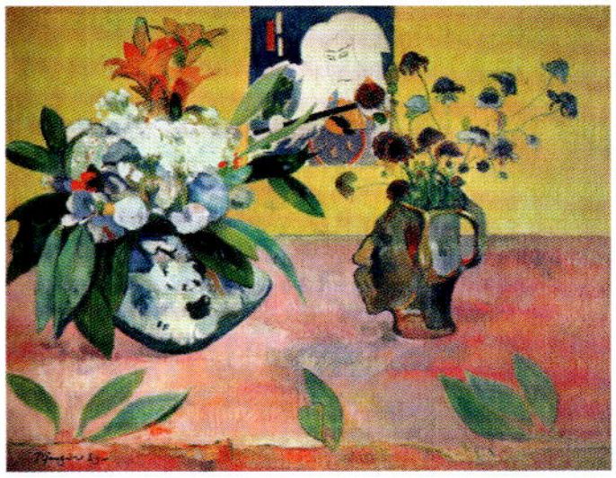

Still life with Japanese Print 1889
Oil on canvas, 85 x 115 cm
Museum of Contemporary Art, Tehran

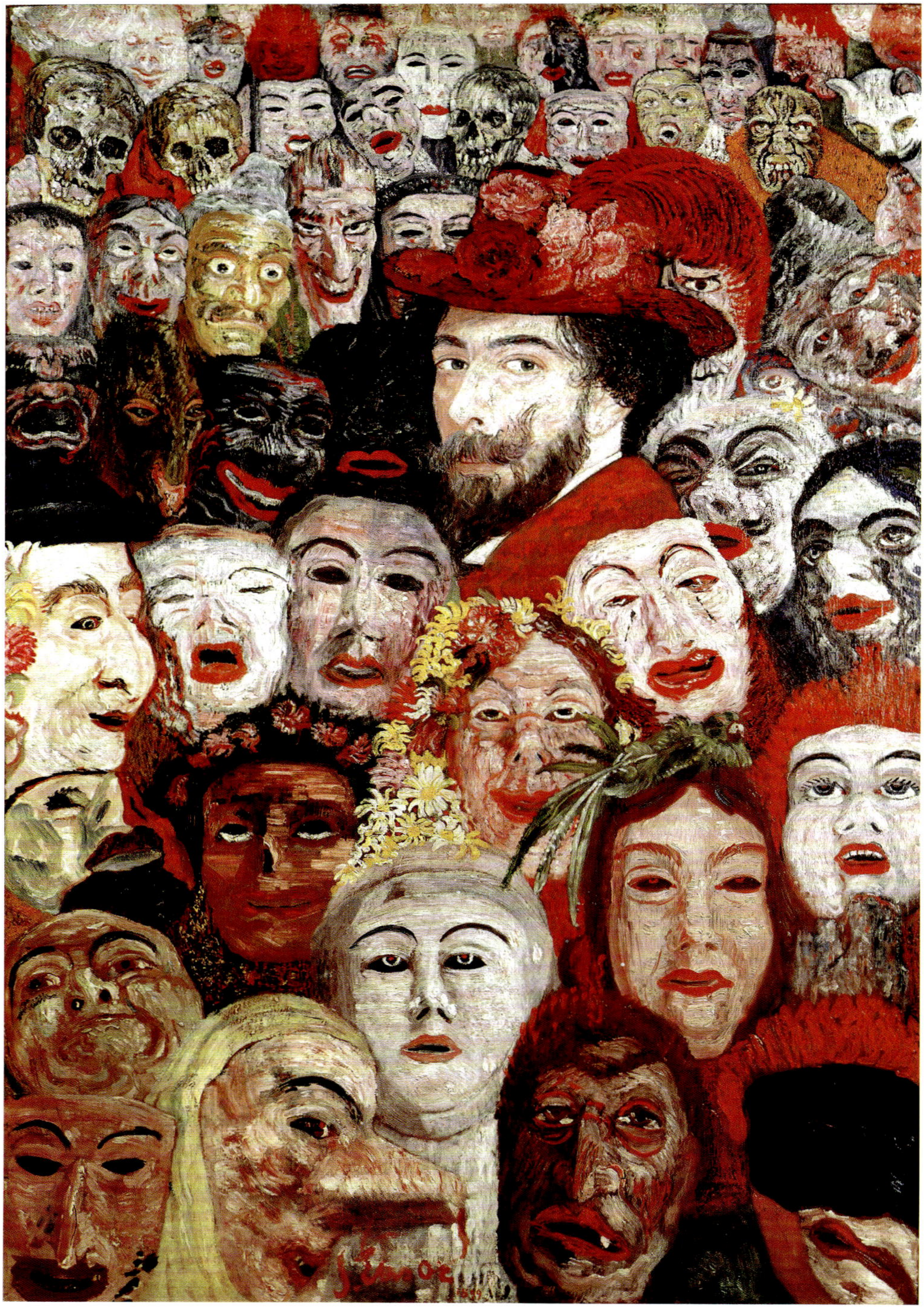

JAMES ENSOR (1860–1949)

Ensor with Masks

For most of his life, Ensor lived in the Belgian seaside town, Ostend. At seventeen he studied at the Académie Royale des Beaux-Arts in Brussels but left after two years, finding the training limited and unstimulating. 'The irate professors capitulated in the face of my audacity,' he said. On returning home to his parents' house he set up a studio in the attic. Downstairs his mother ran a souvenir shop filled with dazzling paraphernalia suitable not only for summer amusement, but also for the spectacle of the town's carnivals. Gradually theatrical motifs such as masks or skeletons started to appear in Ensor's work, as if they existed in normal everyday life. His domestic surroundings were possibly more constricting than his short time at the academy. His family, including his grandmother, his sister and his aunt, provided a highly charged emotional setting in which he attempted to work. Many of his colourful paintings contained notes of caricature, satire and even the grotesque or sinister.

Ensor made many self-portraits. One charcoal drawing is entitled *My Portrait in Sadness and Glory*. His tendency towards the imaginary or fantastic is evident in an early image of himself surrounded by seemingly alive masks. At first it is not obvious that a real face is among them, but his is the only one that is still, calmly looking outwards. The others are menacing and dream-like. The dominance of the colour red spattered across the canvas suggests an uneasy union of make-up and blood.

Ensor did not work in his eccentric home in complete isolation. He remained in touch with the artists he had known in Brussels and for a while adhered to the progressive group Les Vingt which sought to stage exhibitions in Belgium and elsewhere. Recognition came to him late in life after which he was widely admired by younger artists. In 1903 he was named a Knight of the Order of Leopold and went on to become a Baron. Through an unfortunate mistake, his death was once announced on Belgian radio when he was very much alive. Ensor transformed the situation by wearing a black ribbon round his sleeve and declaring, 'I am mourning myself.'

Ensor with Masks 1899
Oil on canvas, 120 x 80 cm
Private Collection

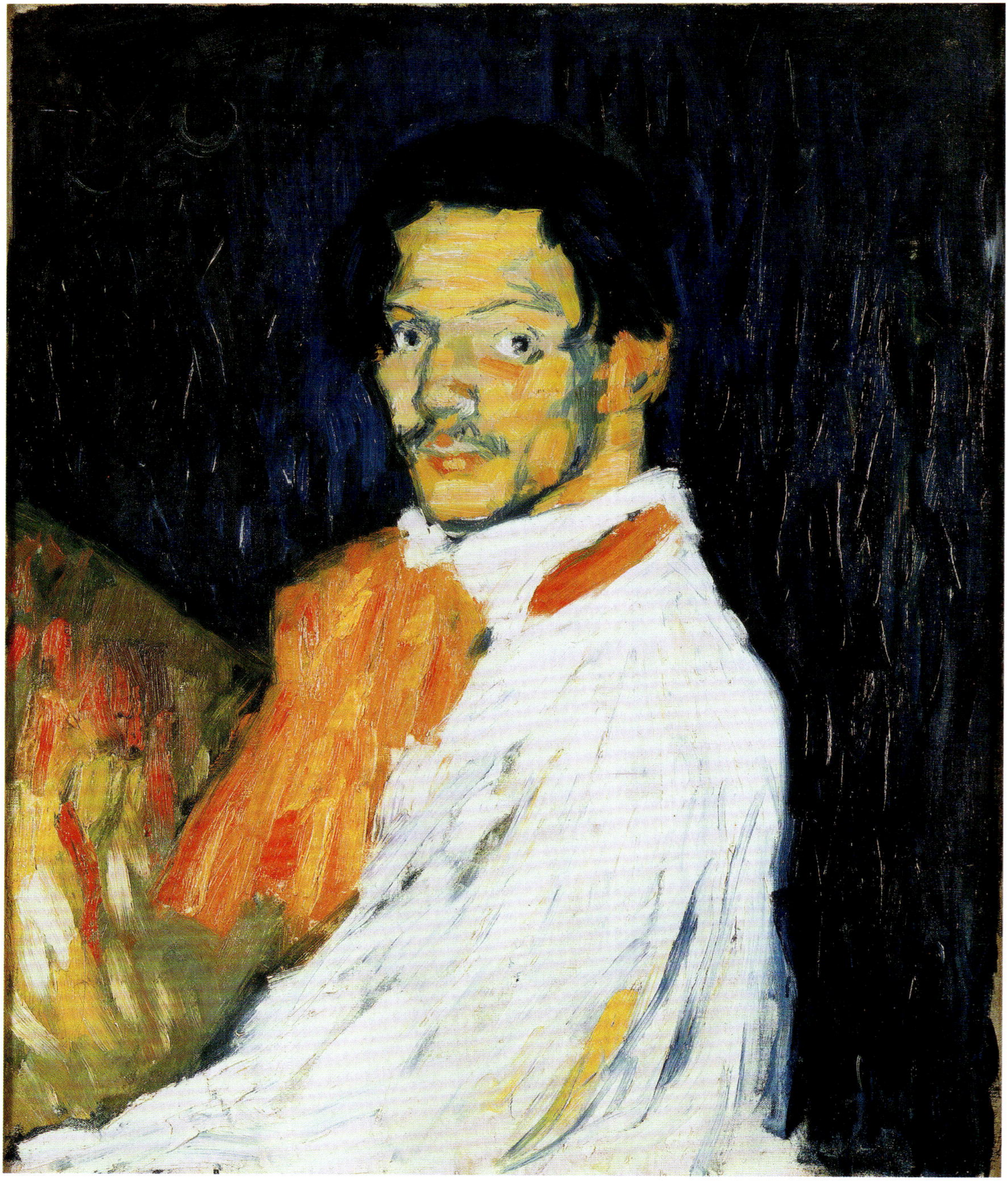

PABLO PICASSO (1881–1973)

Yo, Picasso

In 1901, as a young unknown, Picasso arrived in Paris from Spain. He was about to begin a career that would dominate the art of the coming century. His first significant exhibition was held by the up-and-coming dealer, Ambroise Vollard. Vollard had recently acquired a taste for Spanish artists following his championship of the earlier Impressionists. Picasso had brought with him only a limited number of paintings as well as drawings and pastels. Hurriedly he created more works for the exhibition to adequately represent his ability

This early self-portrait reveals his great self-confidence. By including in its title the words 'Yo, Picasso' (I, Picasso) he compared himself with other great artists of the past. His challenge was also made in the confrontational pose. His round, staring eyes are almost alarming in their *mirada feurte*, their intense gaze, a look that was repeated in later self-portraits. Darkness and light are starkly contrasted, with his artist's smock brilliantly leading to his striking face. The splash of orange in his cravat is repeated in the flesh tones.

At the time Picasso had already become acquainted with several Post-Impressionists whose work he assimilated as he developed his own style. The dark outlining of form and marked brushstrokes of Van Gogh and Toulouse-Lautrec can be detected here. Some years later Matisse painted a portrait of his wife known as *The Green Stripe* after the band of colour down her face. Picasso claimed the idea had originated in this painting where green juxtaposed with orange is reminiscent of colour theory studied by artists in earlier decades.

The theatrical nature of his stance, his look and the bold colouring are all indications of his personality at this time. His lover, Fernande Olivier, wrote her memories of their relationship. She described him as half bohemian, half workman in his dress. He was, 'small, black, thick-set, restless, disquieting, with eyes dark, profound, piercing, strange, almost staring. Awkward gestures, the hands of a woman, poorly dressed, badly groomed. A thick lock of hair, black and shining, slashed across his intelligent and obstinate forehead.'

Yo, Picasso 1901
Oil on canvas, 73.5 x 60.5 cm
Private collection

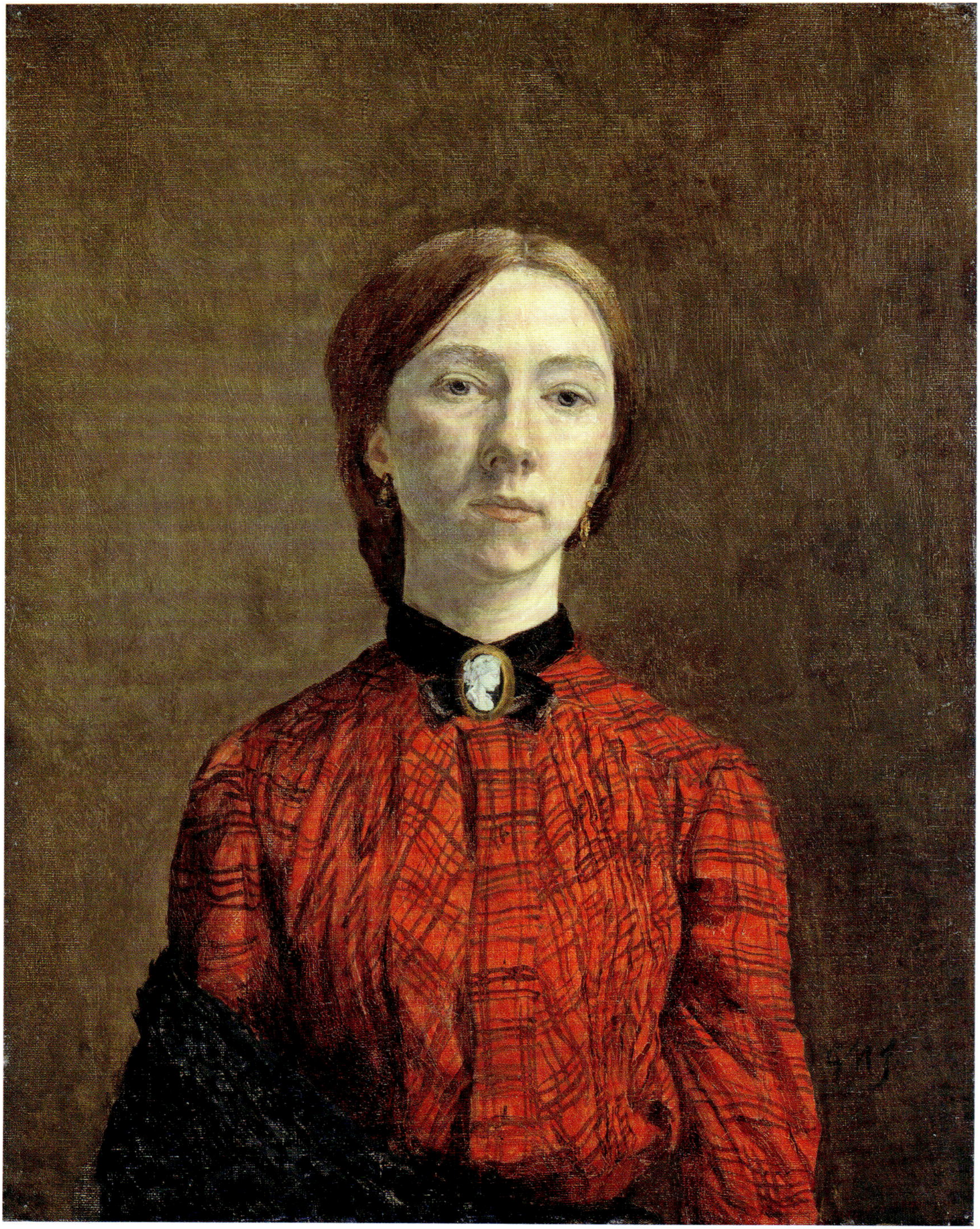

GWEN JOHN (1876–1939)

Self-portrait

The reputation of Gwen John was, for years, overshadowed by that of her bohemian brother, Augustus. Both studied art at the Slade School when it was attended by some of Britain's finest painters of their era. Augustus always encouraged her and, recognising her talent, said he would one day be known as her brother.

For most of her adult life she lived in Paris where, earning a living at first as a model, she bravely sought the freedom to pursue a career in a field that was dominated by men. She studied under Whistler and although new artistic movements were emerging there (such as Cubism and Fauvism) she developed her own style in relative obscurity.

She lived in rented rooms, preferring attics to more spacious areas. Many of her portraits are set in interiors where the light is shadowy and calm. An early self-portrait shows her standing upright, a determined expression on her face. The wide sleeve of her brown blouse matches the lighter tones of her hair within the dark room that surrounds her. A large, jaunty bow is tied beneath her pale face that matches the colour of the hand placed boldly on her hip. Similarly, in her choice of colours for the self-portrait of 1902, she has limited these to pleasing effect. Her face is closer to the picture surface, the flesh and lips tinged with the red of the checked blouse she wears. The tilt of her head, slightly to one side, and her calm expression reveal a serious, questioning nature. The brushstrokes are carefully applied, in layers of glaze, but such detailed work was not easy for her to achieve. She preferred watercolour and compared painting in oils to doing the housework. In her portraits she was able to achieve a profound sense of character through simple compositions of carefully worked tones.

Her celebrated painting of the corner of an attic room in Paris is often viewed as a variant of the self-portrait. She did two versions of the scene. Nobody is there, but the window, her table and an empty chair suggest her absence to be as powerful as her presence.

Self-portrait 1902
Oil on canvas, 44.8 x 34.9 mm
Tate Gallery, London

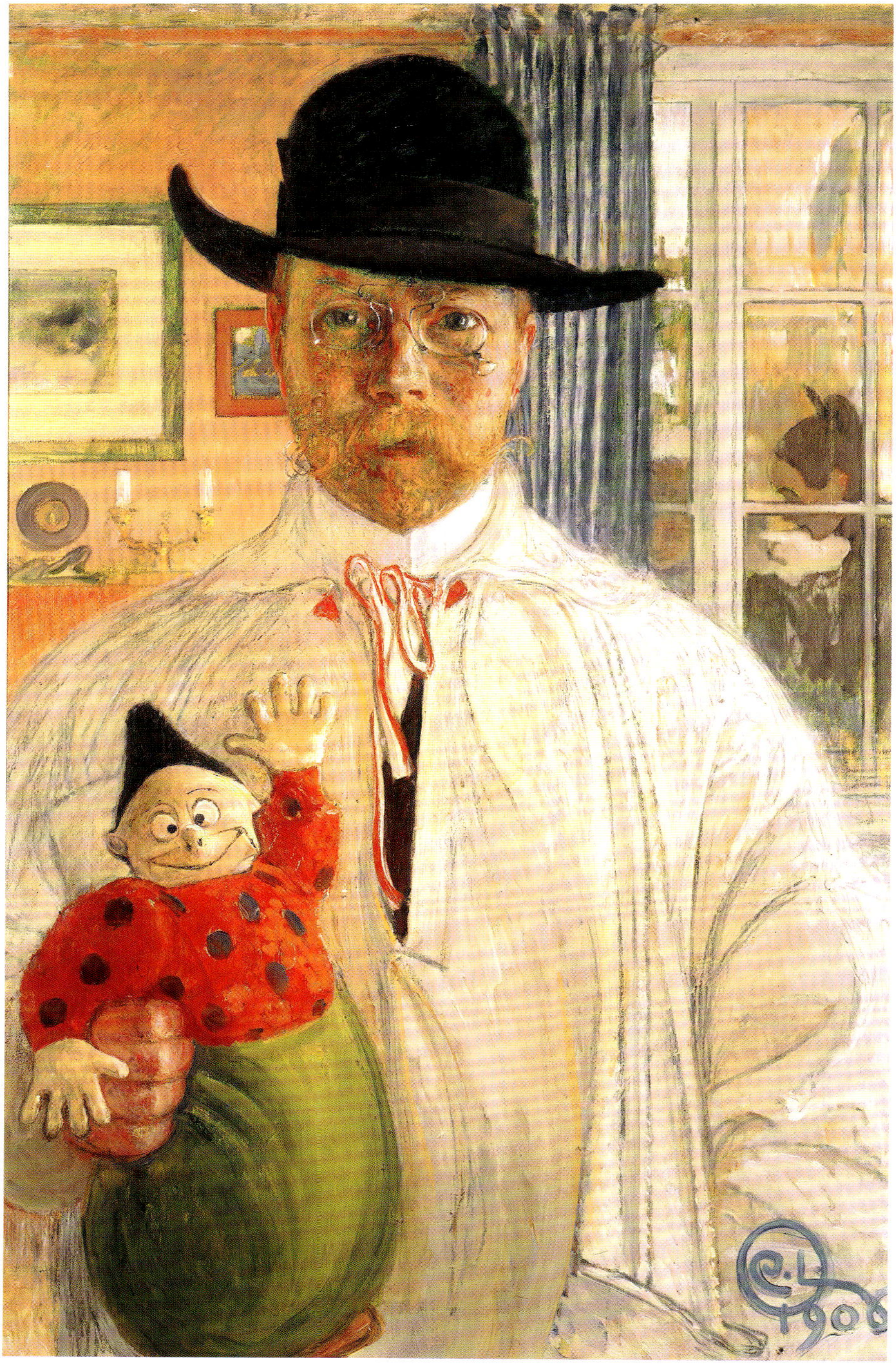
C.L.
1906

CARL LARSSON (1853–1919)

Self-portrait

Larsson's childhood was an unhappy time when he suffered appalling poverty. His father, often absent, is said to have cursed the day he was born. His mother struggled as a laundress to keep her small family alive. Only when he was at school did the prospect of a hopeful future open up to him when a teacher encouraged him to consider art as a career. Following training he became a graphic artist, earning enough to enable him to support his parents. He travelled to Paris in the 1870s when Impressionism had made its mark, but he turned away from the movement, settling for a while with other Swedish artists in the country. Here he met his future wife, Karin, and their union developed not only into a large and happy family life, but into a significant partnership in the development of Swedish interior design.

His popularity is largely due to the many paintings he made of his wife and children in their home which provided an insight into their cheerful personal realm. The fine detail he achieved through linear outline and carefully applied washes of watercolour brought the interiors of their domestic world to life. The family at play, at work, in celebration or attending to the mundane is in contrast to the national theme of the huge painting *Midwinter Sacrifice*, which he considered his most significant work.

Several self-portraits show him at home as father at play or as artist at work. In the portrait where he holds a doll prominently in front of him he is performing neither role, but appears to be demanding the onlooker's attention. He is serious, almost frowning, in contrast to the clownish, gesticulating doll. Both wear dark hats which create stark notes in the general pinkish tone of the picture. Separated from them by a blue striped curtain, a window reveals Karin at work. During their earlier engagement, Larsson had bought the doll for her as he thought it resembled him. The portrait therefore reveals two aspects of his personality. He once said, 'I want to give joy – but not only to one person . . . to everybody.'

Self-portrait 1906
Oil on canvas, 95.5 x 61.5
Uffizi, Florence

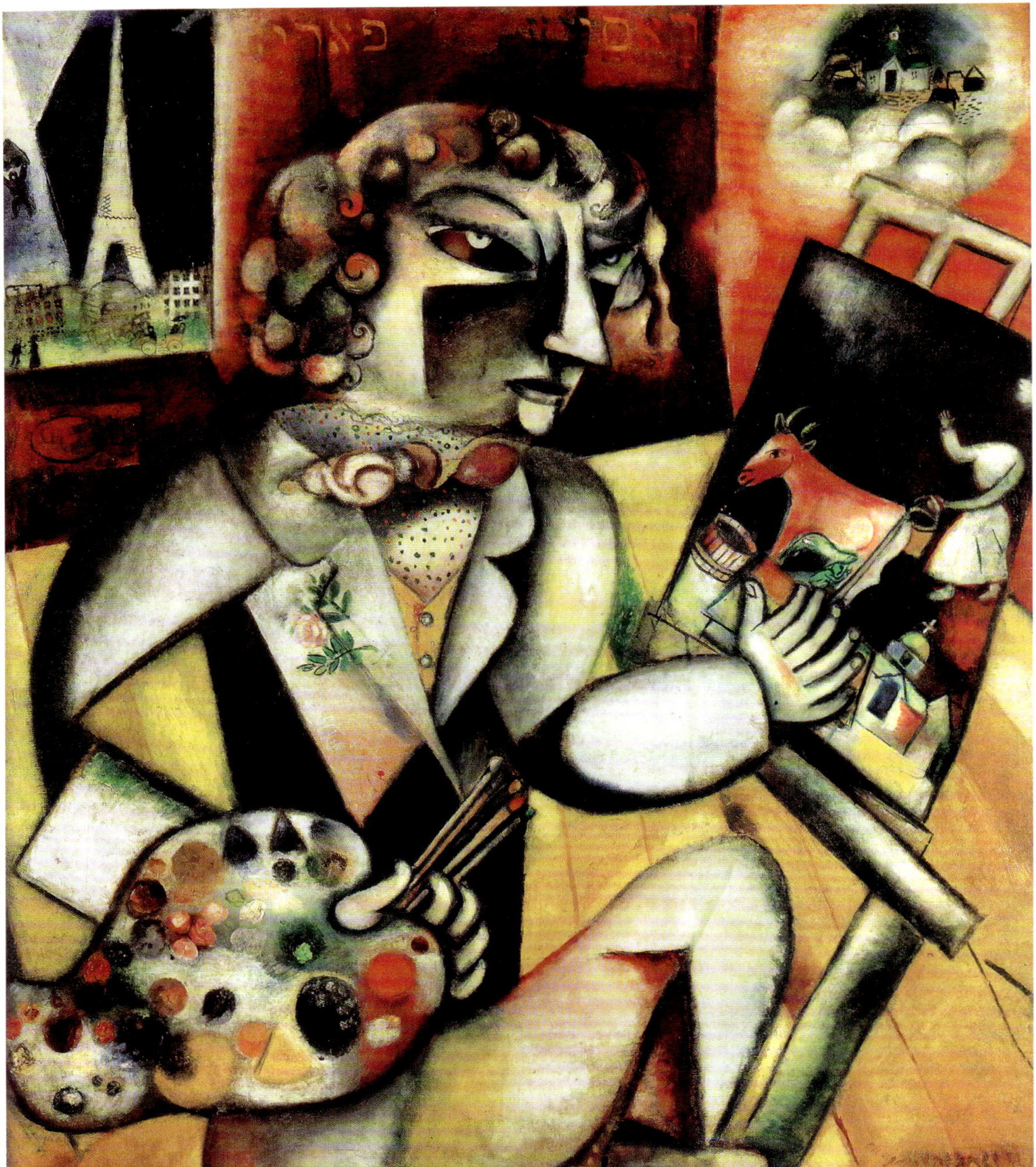

MARC CHAGALL (1887–1985)

Self-portrait with Seven Fingers

Much of Chagall's work contains references to the early part of his life spent in his native Russia. He included not only himself and his family, but also members of the Jewish community in which he had grown up. His training was in Russia, but it was not until he went to Paris for the first time, in 1911, that he was able to witness the significant movements that had flourished there during the first decade of the century. Symbolism, Fauvism and Cubism were to play their parts in his own artistic development. 'I always dreamed of some new kind of art that would be different,' he said, 'In Paris, I at last saw as in a vision the kind of art that I actually wanted to create. It was an intuition of a new psychic dimension in my paintings.'

The puzzling seven fingers he has on his hand in this early self-portrait probably relate to his Jewish identity. The number seven was of mystical significance and associated with God's creation. Here Chagall is himself a creator, an artist with palette and easel in a neat and colourful studio surrounded only by his work. On the wall there is a view of Paris with the Eiffel tower. Is it a window or one of his paintings? The scene at which he is working shows a typical rural scene of his home, informed by affectionate memories. A third image appears, dreamlike, as if on clouds rather than canvas, suggesting the act of creation must first come from within the psyche.

The distorted viewpoints within the painting and the flattened surfaces of the artist's clothes and face show the influence of Cubism and also serve to emphasise the unnaturalistic 'psychic dimension' of his portrait. The bright colouring is the kind that was championed by the Fauves. But Chagall always remained unattached to a specific group. Looking back at this period, years later, he explained it was, 'a time when dreaming was not considered right. Painters were then absorbed in their purely technical researches. One did not speak out loud these dreams.'

Self-portrait with Seven Fingers c.1912–13
Oil on canvas, 126 x 107 cm
Stedelijk Museum, Amsterdam

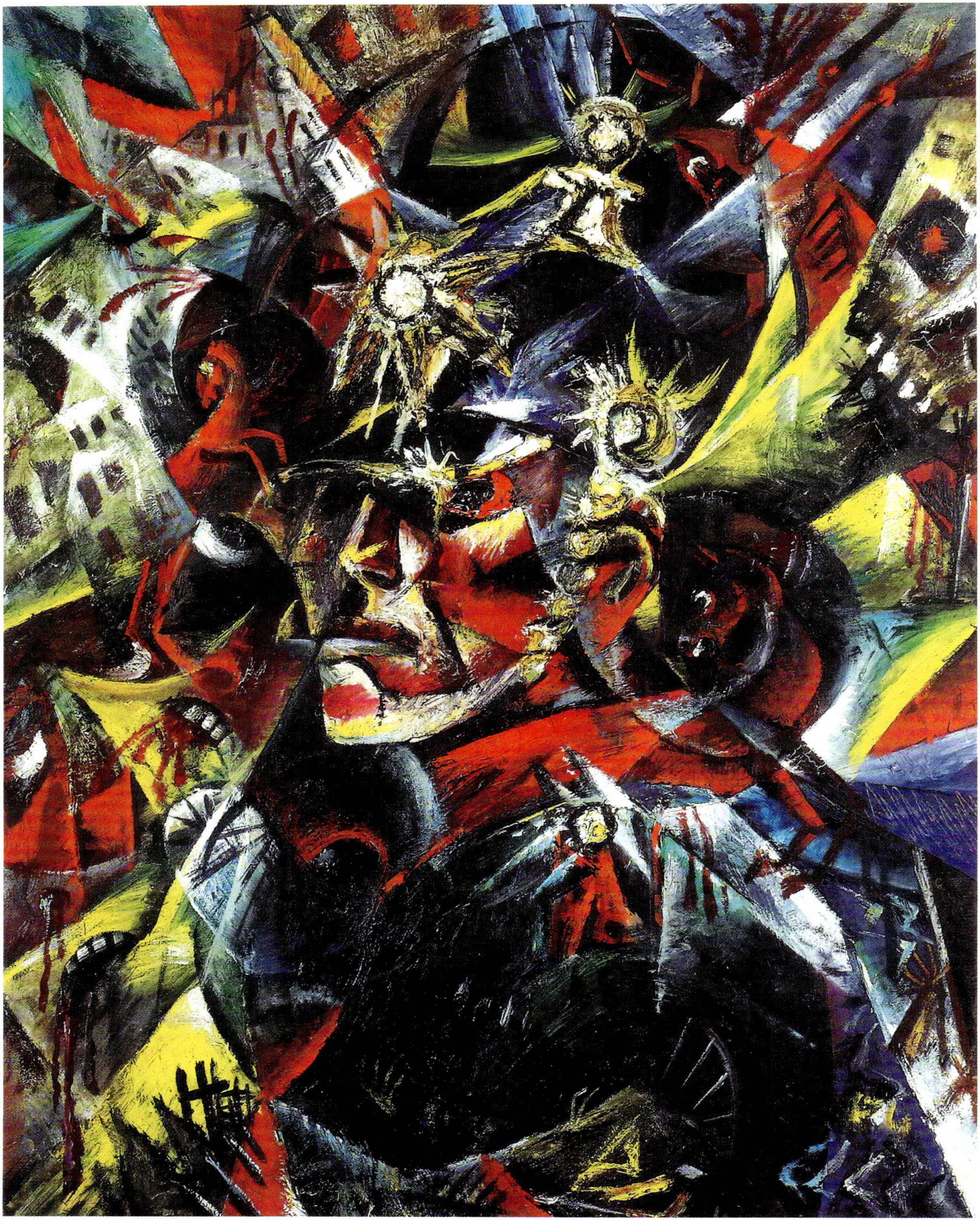

OTTO DIX (1891–1969)

Self-portrait as Mars

The German painter, Otto Dix, is well known for his shocking depiction of Weimar Republic society between the World Wars. He painted crippled veterans, disdainful prostitutes and the fun-loving decadent world of the jazz age. Earlier, at the onset of the First World War, like other idealistic young men, he had been willing to fight and enlisted as a soldier. At the time he had already received artistic training in Dresden and was drawn to his own heritage of the art of the northern Renaissance. He saw an exhibition of Van Gogh's work and became familiar with contemporary trends in the arts which helped form his individual style.

He painted himself as a soldier with an alarming clarity of vision. Portraits 'with a gunner's helmet' or 'as a target' show his willingness to accept the part he played in the early years of the war. 'I had to experience how someone beside me suddenly falls over and is dead and the bullet has hit him squarely,' he said later. 'I had to experience that quite directly. I wanted to.'

In the striking portrait where he identifies himself with Mars, the god of war, he brings to the canvas the distorted perspectives of Cubism and the colourful vitality of Futurism. His head can be detected within a world made up of fragmented, menacing images. Buildings fall, flashes burst, horses go wild yet the strong features of his own chin and nose remain alarmingly still. The appearance of a helmet is formed from carefully placed patches of black together with yellow light as shiny as metal. His war is startling, of primary colours bursting through the dark.

Profoundly moved by his experiences on the frontline, Dix explained: 'As a young man you don't notice at all that you were, after all, badly affected. For years afterwards, at least ten years, I kept getting these dreams in which I had to crawl through ruined houses, along passages I could hardly get through.' A series of prints entitled *War* as well as his large paintings of trenches and battlefields are some of the most realistic and disturbing images of war ever made.

Self-portrait as Mars 1915
Oil on canvas, 81 x 66 cm
Stadtische Kunstsammlung im
Haus der Heimat, Freital

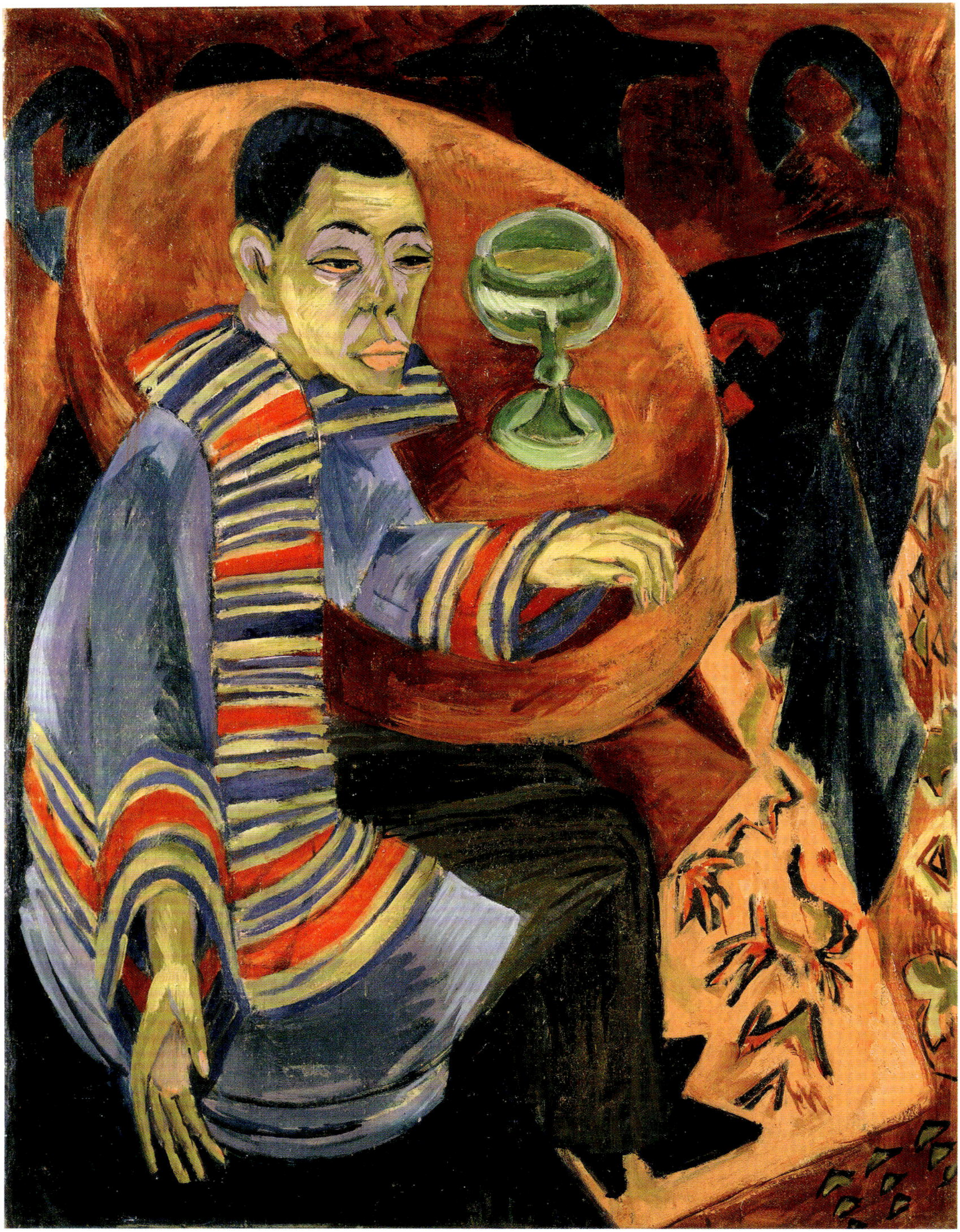

ERNST LUDWIG KIRCHNER

(1880–1938)

The Drinker (Self-portrait)

As a founder member of Die Brücke (the Bridge), Kirchner, together with other artists, looked to both the past and the future, their name symbolising their role between the two. They aimed to find 'freedom of life and action against established and older forces', yet they acknowledged their artistic heritage, admiring, in particular, German woodcut design. They were also interested in so-called primitive art and their choice of distortion and bright colouring aligned them to their Fauve contemporaries in France. Their strong outlines, derived from woodcuts, contributed to a violently emotive style which well represents their form of Expressionism.

In the early period of the First World War, Kirchner, like other German artists, volunteered for military service. During rigourous training he made many revealing yet stark drawings of his fellow soldiers and their barracks life. However, his mental fragility was soon detected and although he never saw active duty on the battlefield, he was granted a temporary discharge followed by several admissions to a sanatorium for psychiatric care.

He created two startling self-portraits in 1915. One showed him as a soldier with an amputated hand and although this was never a reality he had to endure, it served to illustrate the idea of his creativity being cut off. The portrait showing him as a drinker bears no reference to his military activities. Instead, he is an abject figure of disillusionment. Here his open hand seems to demand explanations. His mask-like face betrays the semi-consciousness of the drunk. At the centre of the contrasting blues and reds of the decorative room and the swathing stripes of his clothes, a huge green goblet of absinthe stands centre stage, rigidly upright.

Kirchner suffered a mental breakdown in 1916, more likely due to his excessive drinking and drug abuse than to his experiences of war. He was to make a further dramatic self-portrait 'as a sick person' a few years later where both hands reach up to touch his face. The vivid colours and distorted perspective of the room from which his questioning eyes look out, strengthen the painting's disturbing and emotive content.

The Drinker (Self-portrait) 1915
Oil on canvas, 119 x 89 cm
Germanisches Nationalmuseum, Nuremberg

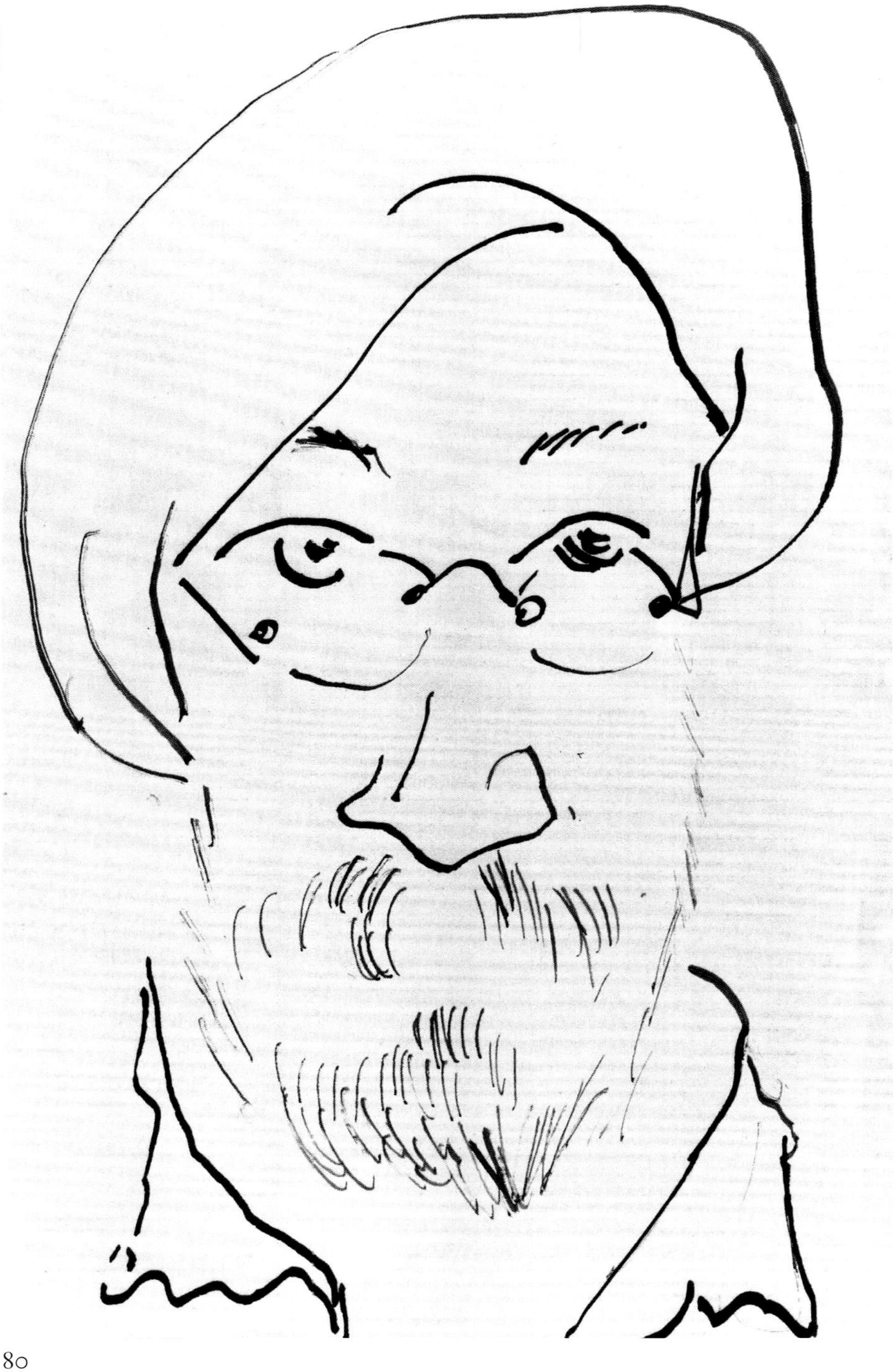

HENRI MATISSE (1869–1954)

Self-portrait

When Matisse exhibited a portrait of his wife, *Woman in a Hat*, in Paris in 1905, he and his fellow painters were labelled 'Fauves' – wild beasts. One critic claimed they had thrown a pot of paint in the face of the public. Matisse had spent months in the south of France, on the Mediterranean, where the bright sunlight had encouraged him to use colour without shadow. Though he knew they were breaking many traditional artistic laws, he felt compelled to pursue his ideas: 'We were at that point like children before nature, and we let our temperaments speak . . . I spoiled everything on principle, and worked as I felt, only by colour.'

Matisse frequently sought the sun, observing the effect its light had upon appearances and how colour became intensified by it. At the same time, drawing was always important for him, not simply to define form or as a preliminary study. The brevity of his line might emphasise the whiteness of paper, in itself a vehicle of light. He described a drawing as an 'orchestration' of simple means. Many of his works are fully detailed drawings, without colour. He also produced etchings and drypoints as well as large lithographs.

He visited Tangier twice where he had trouble finding models willing to pose for him. He was aiming to produce work for a Russian dealer, Sergei Shchukin, and his routine included mornings spent sketching or exploring the heart of the old town while in the afternoons he concentrated on painting. He also did a great deal of horse riding and enjoyed meeting the local people. In this self-portrait he is seen wearing a turban, but does not pretend to be in Moroccan disguise. He has produced a moment's image, almost as a caricature. It may not have come from looking in a mirror. It simply illustrates his present situation, his temporary Moroccan-ness.

'I have always considered drawing not as an exercise of particular dexterity,' he said, 'but as a means deliberately simplified so as to give simplicity and spontaneity to the expression, which should speak without clumsiness, directly to the mind of the spectator.'

Self-portrait c. 1916
Pen and ink on paper,
21 x 13.5 cm
Private collection

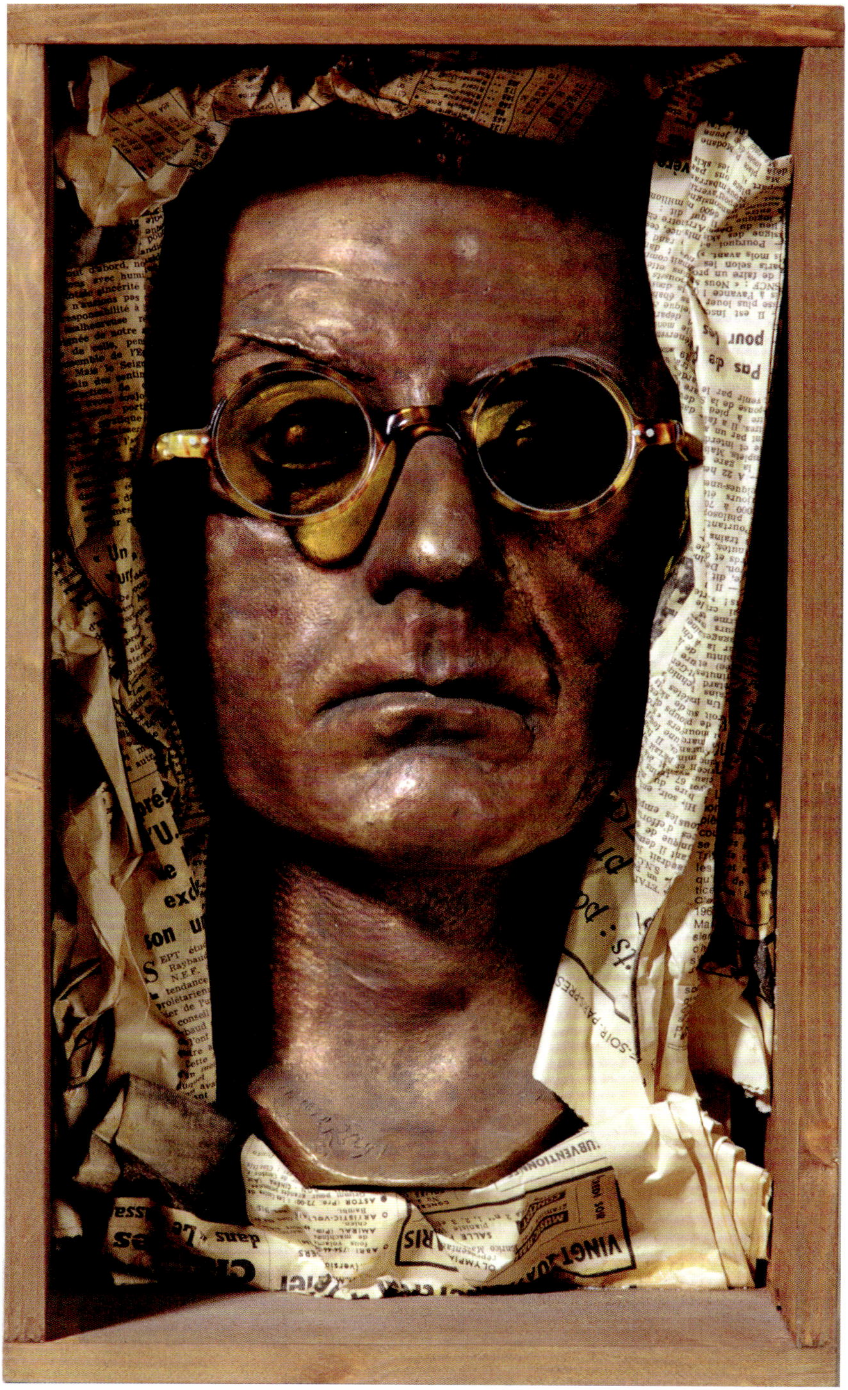
Pas de
pour
VINGT

MAN RAY (1890–1976)

Self-portrait

His real name was Emmanuel Radnitzky but his family adopted the surname Ray due to their awareness of rising anti-semitism. He was nicknamed 'Manny' and eventually the name Man Ray evolved. Early in his career he was attracted to Cubism and worked alongside Marcel Duchamp, whose name is associated with the Dada movement. Ray thought of himself above all as a painter, but once he had moved to Paris he made a significant contribution to the art of photography with the invention of his photograms (which he named 'rayographs' after himself). These were images created without a camera, but where objects arranged on photosensitive paper were exposed to strong light and then processed. Many of his well-known works reveal unexpected effects and were particularly striking in portraits and fashion shots.

The value of objects, especially when placed in unusual juxtapostions with others, was explored by Dada artists and Surrealists. Man Ray made many self-portraits, but one of these is reminiscent of a memento mori, a symbol representing the unavoidable fact of death for each individual. The extraordinary image of this object was intended to be used on the cover of a book of his photographs. Inside a simple, wooden, coffin-like box stands a bronze of Man Ray's unsmiling head. It is partially wrapped in everyday newspaper. This is not a death-mask. The pair of spectacles upon it might suggest the eyes are capable of seeing. 'I have been accused of being a joker,' Man Ray said, 'but the most successful art to me involves humour.'

At the outbreak of the Second World War, Man Ray was forced to return to America where, soon after arriving, he met his wife Juliet, an experienced artist's model. Over thirty years later he died of a lung infection in Paris, the place where he had gained success and which he considered his home. He was buried in Montparnasse. On his tomb Juliet inscribed the words 'unconcerned but not indifferent'. She herself was placed with him at the time of her death where an added slab reads 'together again'.

Self-portrait 1933
Mixed media: bronze, glass, wood, newsprint, 35.7 x 21 x 13.7 cm
Private collection

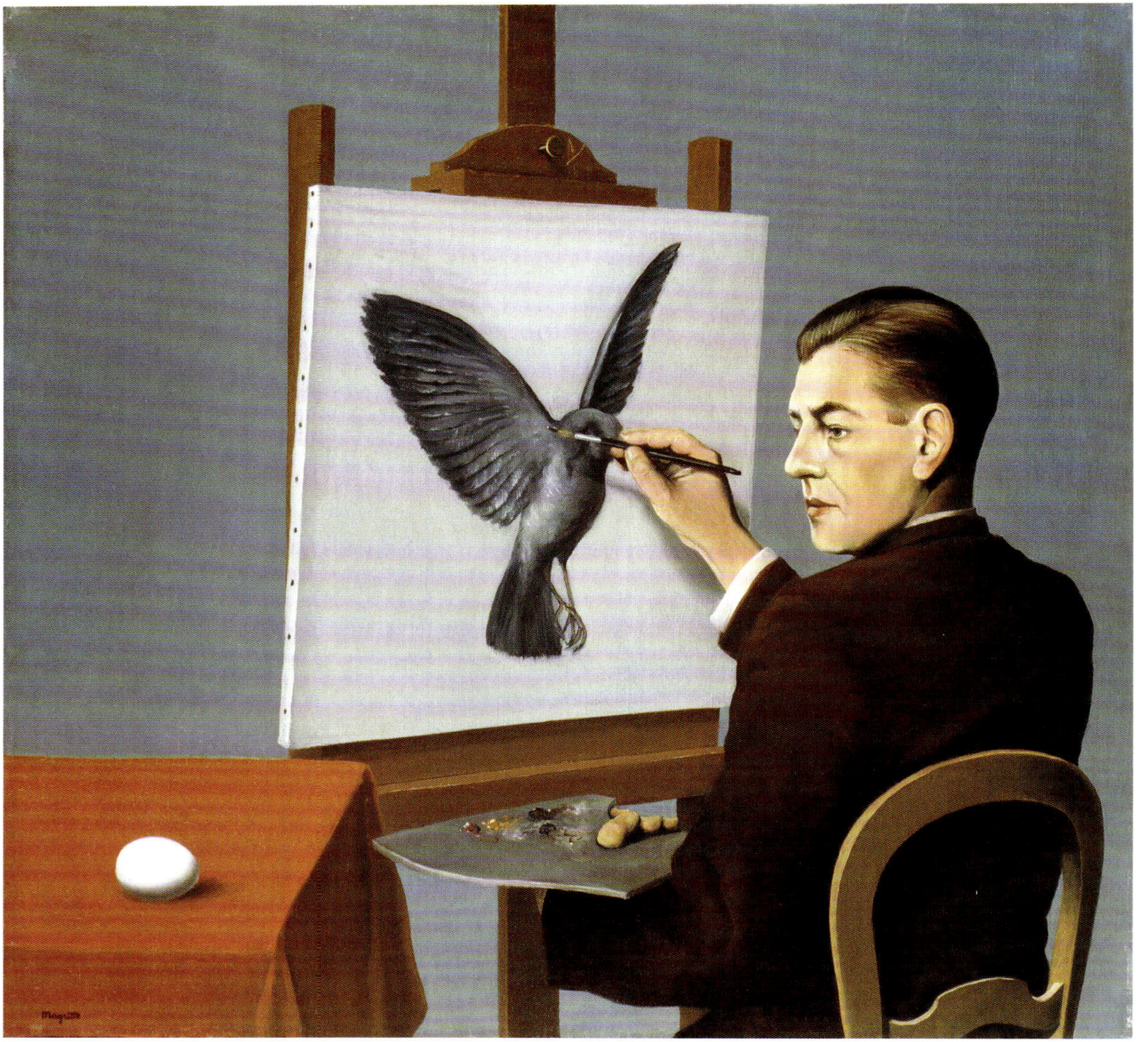

La Clairvoyance 1936
Oil on canvas, 54 x 65 cm
Private Collection

RENÉ MAGRITTE (1898–1967)

La Clairvoyance

Surrealism was a controversial cultural movement that arose between the two World Wars. According to the poet André Breton, its founder member and theorist, its purpose was 'to resolve the previously contradictory conditions of a dream and reality into an absolute reality, a "super-reality"'. As an intellectual movement, it was centred in Paris and consisted mainly of writers and philosophers. However, the work of artists such as Salvador Dali become readily associated with Surrealism. Their visual images, so frequently associated with dreaming, remain memorably perplexing.

The Belgian artist Magritte became a member in the 1920s. He was very fond of the silent movies of his era which depended entirely on the visual to convey dramatic action. In his own paintings he used everyday, familiar images juxtaposed in such a way that they defied any logical kind of reading. His famous picture of a pipe, with the words *Ceci n'est pas une pipe* ('This is not a pipe') written below it, exemplifies his challenging, almost playful attitude. His pipe was in fact a representation of a pipe. 'Painting bears very little direct relation to life,' he said.

In his self-portrait Magritte, like many artists, shows himself at work. His head is realistically portrayed and a good likeness, but what he is painting soon appears to be puzzling. Since he wanted to encourage a new way of looking at objects, he presents each one with simple clarity. The flat colouring of their smooth surfaces and a technique comparable to photography invite legibility. His clean white canvas shows his detailed painting of a bird in flight. But in order to create a likeness of the bird, he does not copy a real one. He is looking at an egg. Our own knowledge of the relation of an egg to a bird is brought into our consciousness. Magritte teases us into considering the impossibility of a rational understanding of the scene. The painting's title adds a further disorientating thought.

Nearly thirty years later he created another painting with the same title. It shows one huge leaf standing upright next to a mature tree.

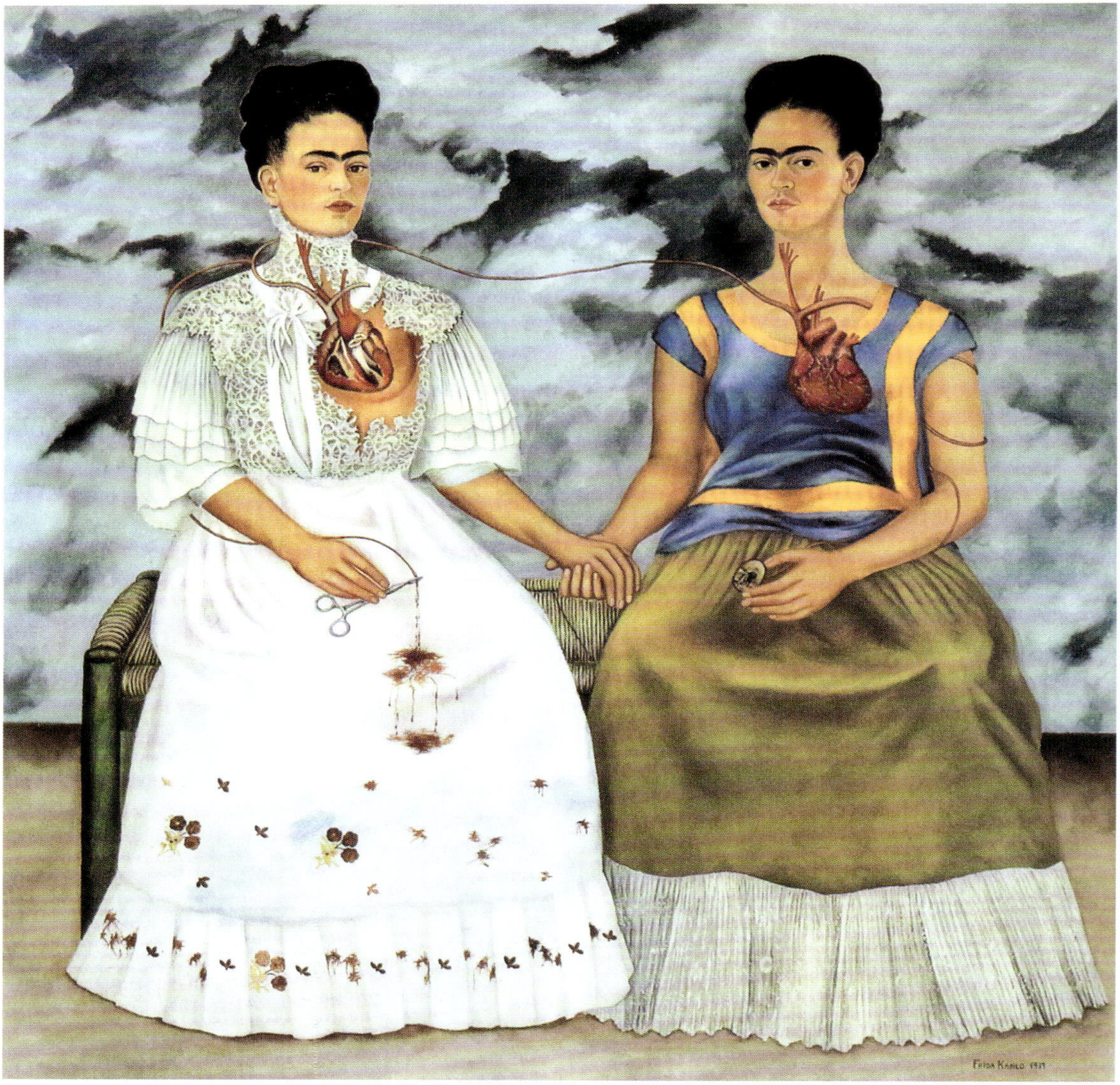

The Two Fridas 1939
Oil on canvas, 173.5 x 173 cm
Museo de Arte Moderno, Mexico City

FRIDA KAHLO (1907–1954)

The Two Fridas

When, as a schoolgirl, Frida Kahlo suffered severe injuries in a road accident, there followed a life of intense pain, periods confined to her bed and repeated hospitalisations. She painted herself more than any other subject, creating a visual autobiography in a frank, colourful and occasionally Surrealistic style. Often she included references to her inherited Mexican culture of which she was intensely proud.

She married a fellow Mexican and celebrated painter, Diego Rivera, about whom she had written, 'My blood is the miracle that travels in the veins of the air from my heart to yours.' After ten years they divorced and Frida painted a portrait of herself as two people. She explained that the painting showed the duality of her personality. She appears on the right in simple Tehuana costume with her heart in tact. In her hand she holds a tiny portrait of Rivera as a child. This was the woman Rivera loved and respected the most. The Frida in white, European dress has a damaged heart that she is attempting to mend with surgical scissors. Pools of blood resembling the red embroidery, continue to form and drip. Despite the hardship of the divorce, the couple remarried the following year.

Frequently she illustrated the physical trauma that her body suffered, including her own birth, the moment of her accident, a miscarriage and when her upper torso was placed in a steel corset. Her strong, facial features are repeatedly portrayed in a three-quarters view from where her eyes, below her dark eyebrows, stare with an almost impassive gaze.

Following further surgery to her spine, in *The Wounded Deer* she likened herself to a hunted animal, attacked by spears, yet still with a smiling face. The deer is in an enclosed space, but it leaps over a green, leafy branch, an indication, perhaps, of her belief in the regeneration of natural life. Although bedridden, she was carried to the first solo exhibition of her work, the year before she died. The last entry in her diary read, 'I hope the exit is joyful – and I hope never to come back – Frida.'

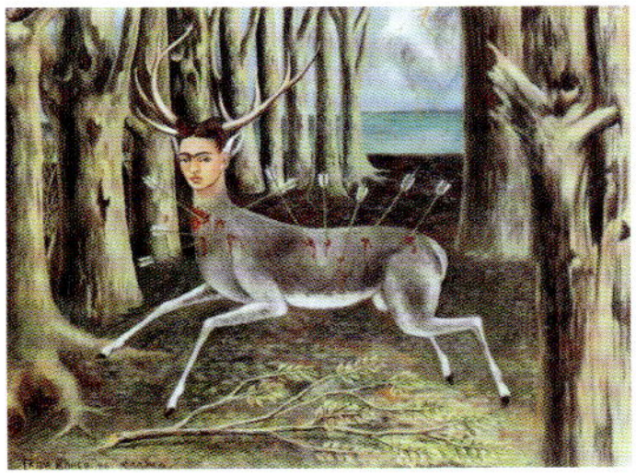

The Wounded Deer 1946
Oil on board, 22.4 x 30 cm
Private collection

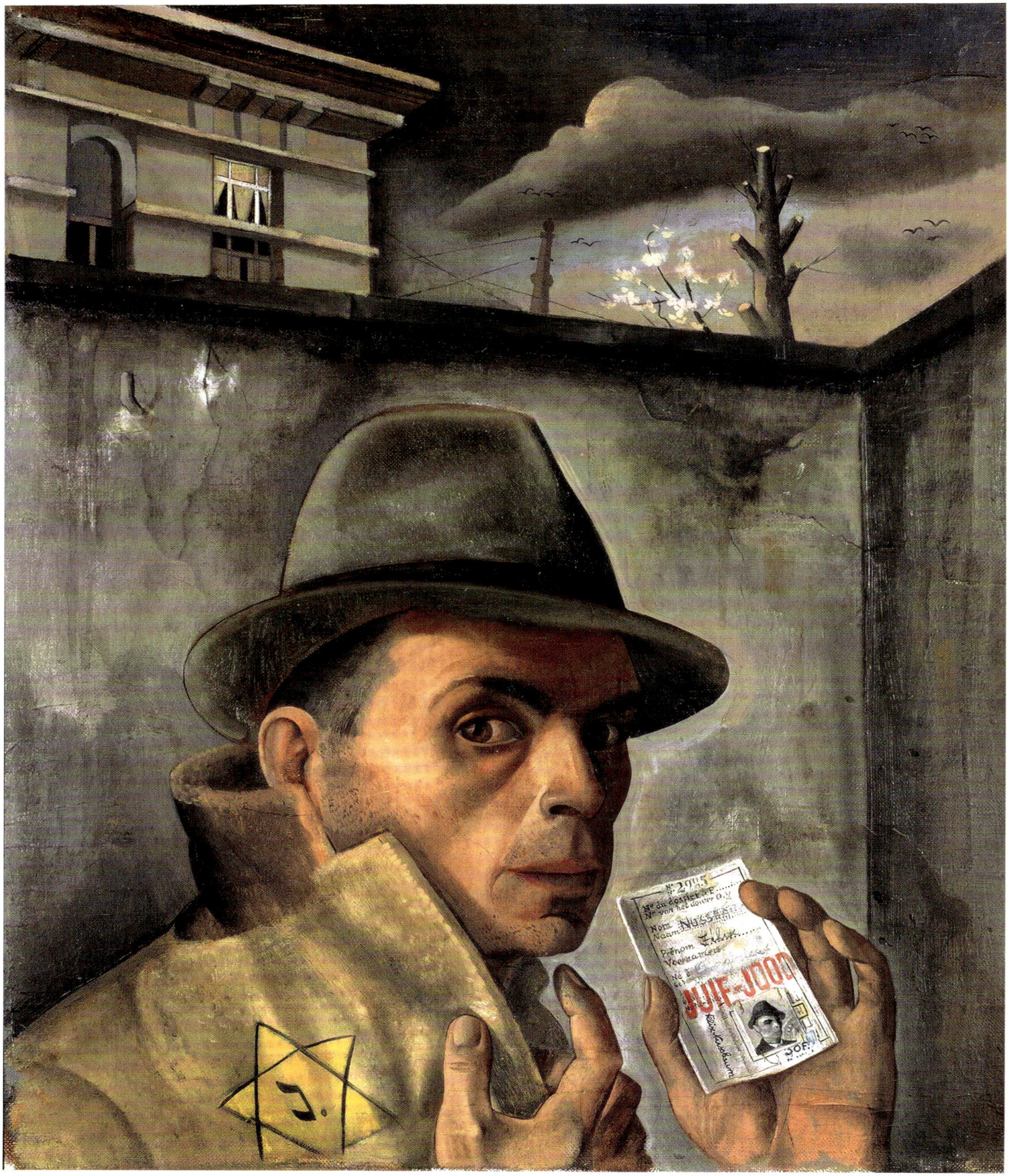
JUIF-JOOD

FELIX NUSSBAUM (1904–1944)

Self-portrait with Jewish Identity Card

The most memorable works created by Nussbaum relate to the terrifying events of his last years. His father, as a patriot, had fought for Germany during the First World War. With a fondness for the arts, he encouraged his son to paint. Following his training, Nussbaum was able to take up a scholarship to study in Rome. During this time the Nazis came to power and Hitler's Ministry of Propaganda was instructed to supervise artistic endeavour. As subject matter, artists were encouraged to emphasise the values of heroism and the supremacy of the Aryan race.

The Nussbaum family were Jews. Reluctantly leaving their homeland, they lived in exile in order to survive. Nussbaum and his new wife made Belgium their base but his parents, unwilling to be separated from Germany, returned there, only to be taken at a later date to Auschwitz. When Nussbaum himself was incarcerated in a camp in France, he signed papers for his return home, then escaped to join his wife. From then on they lived in hiding.

His bleak paintings of this time are haunted by his experiences. Attracted to the symbolic aspects of Surrealism, Nussbaum was able to convey a sense of the psychological isolation and deprivation suffered by the persecuted Jew. He made several self-portraits where his striking face stares, almost accusingly, from each canvas. In the painting of himself with his identity card, his grey felt hat and thick coat collar appear to protect or hide him. Yet his face shows his fear and his hands reveal the objects of his stigmatisation. The yellow badge of the Star of David and the stamped official card explain who or what he has become. He has no other identity.

He stands in a stark, grey, walled area, behind which is a less confined space. Though one tree's branches are cut down, next to it, against a blue patch of sky, another tree is in bloom. Here is a symbol of future life and hope. Nussbaum and his wife were also taken to Auschwitz and killed. A museum in his hometown, Osnabrück, completed in 1998, now has a permanent exhibition of his work.

Self Portrait with Jewish Identity Card 1943
Oil on canvas, 56 x 49 cm
Kulturgeschichtliches Museum, Osnabrueck

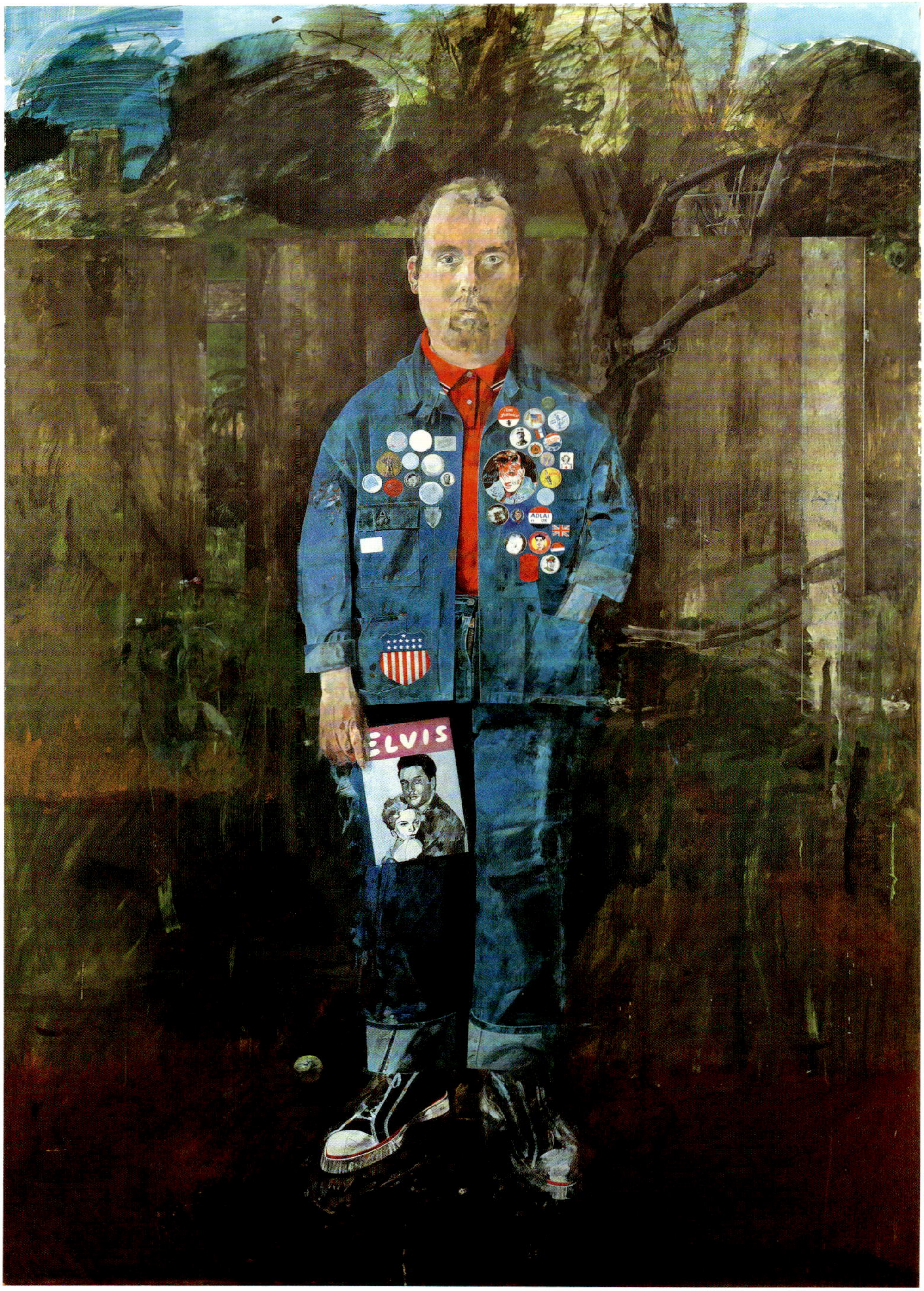
ELVIS
ADLAI

PETER BLAKE (born 1932)

Self-portrait with Badges

Peter Blake's name is always associated with The Beatles. By the time the group's music was known and loved throughout the world, Blake had already become a significant artist of the emerging British Pop Art movement. In the mid-sixties he, together with his American wife, created the sleeve of the band's ground-breaking album, *Sgt. Pepper's Lonely Hearts Club Band*. A collage of lifesize cardboard cutouts of over sixty famous people were placed round the group who stood at the centre of the cover image.

Years earlier Blake had won an award for the latest of several self-portraits he had made. The depiction is reminiscant of the pose of Gainsborough's *Blue Boy*, but Blake is dressed in hard-worn contemporary denim rather than fancy silk. Blake's pose is also similar to Watteau's *Gilles* who, as the member of a group of actors, appears serious, aware of the Pierrot costume he wears. The clothes are important in all three works and Blake's denim pieces were no fancy dress but his own clothes, bought at different times. The background where Blake stands is no eighteenth-century sylvan setting, but a mundane garden fence. Hurrying to complete the painting for entry to the competition, Blake did not have time to include the garden's flower bed.

He stood before a mirror to paint most of the figure but placed the jacket and its badges on a dummy from which he worked. Normally he would only wear one or two badges, but for the portrait he included many. Some of these, together with the baseball boots, the Elvis fan magazine as well as the size of the US flag (compared to the tiny Union Jack) lay emphasis on America rather than Britain. The inclusion of such accessories serve as clues, acting as a traditional means of identifying the subject's own interests. Though he didn't visit the States until later, Blake was already impressed by America's dynamic popular culture.

Right up until 2013 Blake has created album sleeves for artists including The Who, Band Aid, Eric Clapton, Oasis and Madness. In 2002 he was knighted for his services to art.

Self-portrait with Badges 1961
Oil on board, 174.3 x 121.9 cm
Tate Gallery, London

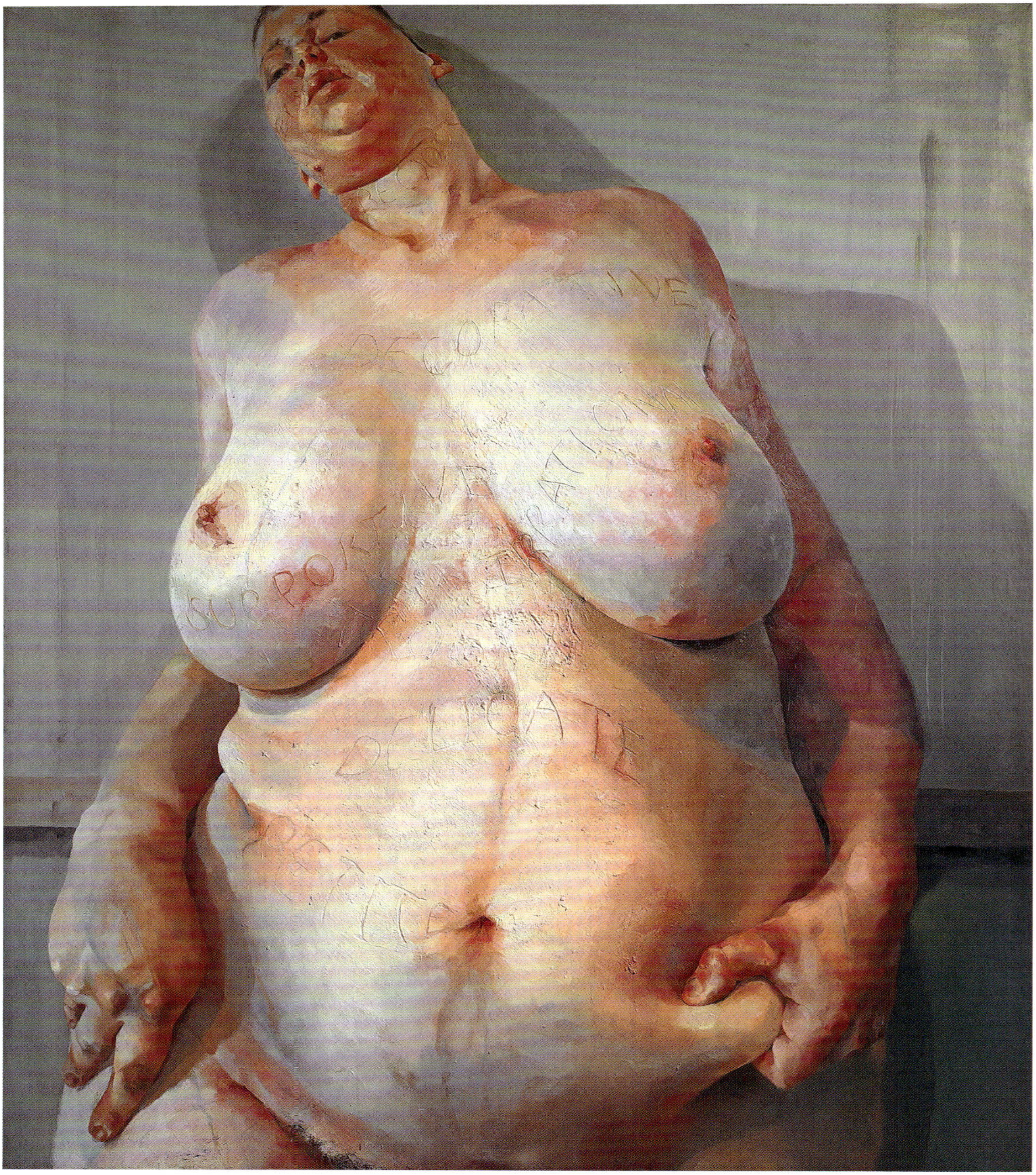
SUPPORTIVE
DELICATE

JENNY SAVILLE (born 1970)

Branded

The female nude has always been a favoured subject for artists, ever since the creation of images first began. Thousands of years ago, during the prehistoric era, naked women were represented in small, stone statuettes. Though later called 'Venus' figures, their true relevance is uncertain but may relate to religious or ritualistic activities. In more modern times, the image of a nude woman, whether in sculpture or painting, has embodied notions of maternity, fertility and, above all, ideal beauty.

Jenny Saville questioned these ideas and in the current of feminism, challenged their history. Her large paintings of female bodies brought their nudity on to the butcher's block. With a dexterous handling of oil paint, she imitated the nature of flesh, including its blemishes, choosing poses that were often distorted or deliberately confrontational.

On finishing her training at Glasgow School of Art in 1992, all the work in her final degree show was sold. Charles Saatchi, the art collector and gallery owner, tracked down the sold items and went on to commission Saville for more work that he hoped to include in his own collection. This led to the astounding success of her early career.

In *Branded* the huge breasts and belly of the body seem exaggerated, given the angle from which they appear to be painted. The tones of the skin, similar to the background, resemble bruising. The figure's left hand clasps her flesh as if to demonstrate its excess while her right hand looks unhealthily swollen. Placed at a distance, above the folds of her chin, is the face of Saville herself, staring down the great body as if to challenge any adverse reaction.

Why paint a figure with such shocking realism? On the surface of the skin, disguised in the mottled colouring, words can be found as clues to the painting's meaning. 'Supportive', 'Precious', 'Delicate' and 'Petite' are all adjectives that can be applied to conventional ideas of the female. Saville's female nude is a daring invitation to step back and to consider the art of the past in the light of contemporary thought.

Branded 1992
Oil and mixed media on canvas,
209.5 x 179 cm
Private collection

INDEX

Artists whose self-portraits appear in the book are in *italic*.

ACKNOWLEDGEMENTS

The Publishers would like to thank those listed below for permission to reproduce the artworks illustrated in this book and for supplying photographs. Every care has been taken to trace copyright holders. Any copyright holders we have been unable to reach are invited to contact the publishers so that a full acknowledgment may be given in subsequent editions.

COVER, PAGE 11 LEFT Royal Academy of Arts, London / Bridgeman Art Library PAGE 1, 36 courtesy National Gallery of Art, Washington, gift of Mr and Mrs Robert Woods Bliss, 1949.6.1 PAGE 8 © The Munch Museum / The Munch-Ellingsen Group, BONO, Oslo / DACS, London / Museum of Fine Arts, Houston, Texas, gift of Louisa Stude Sarofim in memory of Alice Pratt Brown / Bridgeman Art Library PAGE 10 De Agostini Picture Library / G. Dagli Orti / Bridgeman Art Library PAGE 11 RIGHT Dublin City Gallery, The Hugh Lane, Dublin / Bridgeman Art Gallery PAGE 12 © DACS, London 2014 PAGE 13 © David Hockney PAGE 14 courtesy National Gallery of Art, Washington, Samuel H. Kress Collection, 1957.14.125 PAGE 20 The Art Archive / Mondadori Portfolio/Electa PAGE 26 Vatican Museums and Galleries, Vatican City / Alinari / Bridgeman Art Gallery PAGE 28 Museum of Fine Arts, Boston, Emma F. Munroe Fund. Inv. 60.155. All rights reserved / Scala, Florence PAGE 30 Victoria and Albert Museum, London / Bridgeman Art Library PAGE 40 © Tate, London PAGE 41 Bridgeman Art Library PAGE 42 akg-images / Erich Lessing PAGE 46 National Gallery, London / Scala, Florence PAGE 48 Academia San Fernando, Madrid / Scala, Florence PAGE 50 Ashmolean Museum, University of Oxford / Bridgeman Art Library PAGE 52 The Art Archive / Bibliothèque des Arts Décoratifs Paris / Gianni Dagli Orti PAGE 54 akg-images / Archives CDA PAGE 56 Bibliothéque Nationale de France, Département des Estampes de la Photographie, Paris PAGE 57 courtesy National Gallery of Art, Washington, Horace W. Goldsmith Foundation through Robert and Joyce Menschel, 2000.21.1 PAGE 60 akg-images PAGE 65 Giraudon / Bridgeman Art Library PAGE 66 White Images / Scala, Florence / © DACS, London PAGE 68 Art Resource / Scala, Florence / © Succession Picasso/DACS, London PAGE 70 © Tate, London PAGE 72 Photo Scala, Florence, courtesy of the Ministero Beni e Att. Culturali PAGE 74 © Chagall ® / © ADAGP, Paris and DACS, London PAGE 76 © DACS, London PAGE 78 Scala, Florence PAGE 80 © Succession H. Matisse/ DACS, London PAGE 82 Private collection / Peter Willi / Bridgeman Art Library / © Man Ray Trust / ADAGP, Paris and DACS, London PAGE 84 Scala, Florence / © ADAGP, Paris and DACS, London PAGE 86, 87 © Banco de México Diego Rivera Frida Kahlo Museums Trust, Mexico, D.F./ DACS, London PAGE 88 Photo Scala, Florence / BPK, Bildagentur fuer Kunst, Kultur und Geschichte, Berlin / © DACS, London PAGE 90 © Tate, London / Peter Blake. All rights reserved, DACS, London PAGE 92 Photo Christie's Images / Bridgeman Art Library © Jenny Saville. All rights reserved / DACS, London PAGE 96 © Juliet Heslewood

JULIET HESLEWOOD studied History of Art at London University and later gained an MA in English Literature at Toulouse. For over twenty-five years she lived in France where she devised and led study tours on art and architecture as well as continuing her writing career. Her books include *Mother: Portraits by 40 Great Artists*, *Lover: Portraits by 40 Great Artists* and *The History of Western Painting* for young people which has been translated into twelve languages. Juliet now lives in Oxfordshire where she continues to write on both art and folklore and is a freelance lecturer in History of Art.

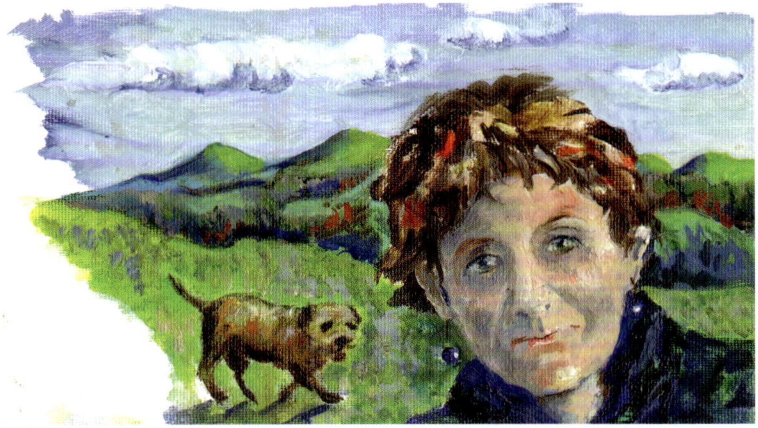

Self-portrait of the Author: I've always loved singing, writing and painting. My artistic heroes are Paul Gauguin, Lennon/McCartney, the Brontë sisters and Edward Elgar. My favourite occupation is to walk in open countryside with my dog.